MOOD THERAPY

The Essential Guide to Stabilizing Your Mood, Learn Expert Tips and Advice on How to Manage Your Moods, Stay Positive in Life, Re-appreciate life and Take back your smile

By

GARY FIKE

TABLE OF CONTENTS

INTRODUCTION

Often life passes us by so fast that it feels as though we are resting in a train with our life sliding by like the landscapes outside the window. We feel like we have no selection however to oblige the guidelines others set for us.

Bad days happen. A flopped job meeting, a broken coffee machine (when you truly need coffee), -- we understand, life can sometimes draw. We can't get rid of an excruciating colleague or a dreadful commute (sorry),.

Some days staying favorable and upbeat can feel like an uphill struggle. Maybe it was a stressful day at the workplace, a fight with a buddy, or even simply an off day-- whatever it is, there are most definitely points you can do to improve your state of mind.

And also it's not surprising that tiffs can slip up on us so often. According to psycho therapist Guy Winch, author of the book Emotional First Aid: Healing Rejection, Guilt, Failure, and Other Everyday Hurts, a tiff can be triggered by anything from shame over failing to remember a person's birthday celebration, to impressive tasks on our to do list, to not getting sufficient likes on a important or personal Facebook share. Essentially, human beings are delicate animals, and also it's not abnormal or perhaps uncommon for little points to obtain us in a funk.

Some days are just ... negative days. Several of them start great and slowly degrade with time, and others are truly terrible from the get-go. You awaken in a horrifically horrible mood for whatever reason, or you spill coffee premises while trying to make a cup (yes, that has occurred to me), or you think you're entrusting a lot of time, just to end up in countless bumper-to-bumper web traffic. Some days, it just seems like you have no selection but to kick things off on the wrong side of the bed.

What's more, according to a psychology research study included on ABC News, while a portion of our individual happiness is pre-determined by genes and situation, research reveals that as much as 40 percent can be controlled throughout daily ideas and activities.

This means that there are most definitely a variety of aggressive things we can do when we start feeling ourselves getting down.

WHAT ARE MOODS?

Good and negative moods are personalities to have emotions utilizing the exact same devices.

You recognize the difference between being in a good mood when you often tend to be happy and also pleasant, and being in a poor mood when you have a tendency to be sad and also grumpy. Moods have a tendency to be much extra long-lasting, going for hours or days, whereas an emotion may just last minutes. Second, feelings are concerning something specific, such as a person or situation, however state of minds are a lot extra scattered with no identifiable item.

Emotions and also moods are connected. When you are in a tiff, you are inclined to have unfavorable emotions such as being depressing, mad, or afraid concerning something. But when you are in an excellent mood, you are inclined to have favorable feelings such as being hopeful or happy concerning something. The nature of emotions must inform us concerning the nature of moods.

According to the semantic reminder concept of feelings, feelings are patterns of firing in huge teams of nerve cells that incorporate neural depictions of situations, cognitive evaluations of those situations, and also physical adjustments (Thagard and Schröder,

2014, Thagard 2018). For instance, being happy that you get on vacation is a mind procedure that binds together your neural depictions of (1) the vacation, including both words and photos, (2) your evaluation that the holiday is achieving your goals such as enjoying, and (3) changes in your body such as raised heart rate and lower cortisol.

However what are moods that run without representations of certain situations? I propose that moods are dispositions to have feelings. Salt has a disposition to liquify in water, and also glass containers have a disposition to break when gone down. What is a disposition?

Philosophers often deal with dispositions as counterfactual conditional (Choi & Fara, 2012). To say that a teaspoon of salt has a disposition to dissolve in water is to say that if it had actually been put in water after that it would certainly have dissolved. Sadly, the basic thoughtful method of handling such counterfactuals remains in regards to feasible globes. To claim that the salt would certainly have liquified is to say that there is some feasible globe similar to ours in which it does liquify.

This characterization of personalities in terms of counterfactuals and possible worlds is ineffective both emotionally and literally. It reveals no understanding of the physics of salt, and also taps into odd metaphysics concerning feasible globes rather than right into the psychology of just how people think about personalities.

A much better method of understanding counterfactuals originates from the expert system researcher Judah Pearl (2000). He says that you can assess a counterfactual by taking into consideration a causal version that shows how different elements interact with each various other. The mechanism of solubility of table salt is well understood since we recognize that sodium chloride results from binding positive sodium atoms with unfavorable chlorine atoms. When salt is area in water, the ions separate. If it does not in fact obtain placed in water, knowledge of these mechanisms justifies the conclusion that salt is soluble also. When we recognize underlying devices that forecast the results of various manipulations, we have reason to think that a counterfactual is true.

State of mind isn't only what makes us smile or laugh aloud. Usually, it's relevant to an outside thing (scenario, location, other individuals, etc.) or inner ideas.

It refers specifically to internal feelings, which are subjective. It doesn't cover the outside symptom of the feelings. When we think about inner feelings and their external expression, we're describing revealing affection, not state of mind.

Being in a good mood implies being happy.

We usually hear individuals say "I'm in an excellent mood" or "I'm in a tiff". We state these things when we want to share our way of thinking on certain scenarios. Our vital and nostalgic senses are enhanced when we're in an excellent mood. Namely, we feel happy and agree with all the positive events that are taking place.

If we're in a good state of mind, we're positive and want to do things. We tend to decrease setbacks by minimizing them, due to the positive outlook that our good state of mind generates.

We do not want to be with various other people when we're in a negative state of mind.

On the various other hand, when we locate ourselves in a negative mood, we're cynical and really feel passive. We're cold and lack any rate of interest in anything that needs minimal effort.

In this sense, setbacks might seem aggravating and impossible troubles. This has a tendency to intensify our mood even much more. We choose that others leave us alone and not trouble us when we're in a negative state of mind.

Similarly, the personality of state of minds to create unfavorable or favorable emotions is the outcome of the hidden mechanisms that create feelings. Remaining in a state of mind is having processes going on in your body, and also in your mind's subconscious evaluations of circumstances, that together generate certain sort of feelings in feedback to particular kinds of circumstances. If you are in a great mood, then your physiology and background thinking are running in means that incline you to translate brand-new circumstances favorably. Extra particularly, if you have a few of the physical hallmarks of excellent feelings such as secure heart prices, breathing rates, and cortisol levels, and if you have been making mainly positive assessments regarding things, then these background processes stood for in your mind will certainly make you more likely to reply to brand-new situations with positive emotions.

So state of minds can be comprehended in regards to the exact same mind devices as feelings.

WHAT FACTORS CAN AFFECT YOUR MOODS

There are numerous elements that can impact our state of minds. The foods that we consume, the duty workout plays, the social interactions we surround ourselves with, and the ideas and habits we have can all lead to lows in state of mind that can injure our productivity.

By maintaining a healthy balance of physical task, nutrition, self-care principles, leisure time and also social communications, we are much better able to crush an adverse state of mind and also fight back when one strategies. By believing of the points that are remarkable in our lives and also allowing those characteristics to boost our spirits and also help put things in correct point of view, we are able to be a lot more positive each day and knowledgable of when an unfavorable state of mind hits and just how ideal to conquer it.

Some aspects are exterior and come from the surrounding setting in a person's life. Other elements are inner and originate from inside. These appear in the type of physical or psychological sensations or as a combination of both.

There's no way to appropriately categorize the variables that influence our state of mind. This is because one of their fundamental qualities is that they're particular per individual. Simply put, everyone is sensitive to certain factors in a specific method.

Thus, the same circumstances can influence different people in different means, according to their character and also personality. In order to examine this out, we can try a straightforward experiment that contains going to a celebration and also quiting to observe each of the guests. Particularly, we're trying to regard everyone's state of mind and predominant state of mind. Probably, we would certainly see someone that's happy, radiant, talkative, and enthusiastic.

Right here are eleven points that can be tinkering our state of minds and exactly how best to deal and to get back to being more confident and also energized.

1. You Are "Hungry".

Sometimes we get in a tiff simply because we require food," states diet professional Keri Gans, MS, RDN, CDN, that is additionally a speaker for America's Better Sandwich over e-mail with Bustle. "The term 'hangry'-- becoming angry, irritated or aggravated due to the fact that you are hungry-- describes it well. Whether it be a snack or a dish make sure what you eat is well balanced," she includes. It's finest to eat something with protein, complex carbohydrates and healthy and balanced fats, integrated, rather than something sweet or refined.

2. Not Recovering After Exercise.

While workout is excellent for increasing endorphins and also improving our moods, if not offered time to recoup and fix, our muscle mass can hurt and our moods may be endangered. "Refuel and moisturize with a little protein, a little carb, and a little fat," claims running coach and individual instructor Susie Lemmer, over e-mail with Bustle. A banana with nut butter, a yogurt with berries and also almonds, or a sandwich with poultry and avocado will work.

3. Your Menstrual Cycle.

For people with periods, menstruation cycles can seriously impact our state of minds. Hormonal agent variations can influence our emotions, leading us to feel happier at certain minutes in our cycle and even more unfavorable, short-tempered, hungry and also worn down throughout others. When we are on our periods, we may experience enhanced adverse emotions, so it's vital to be careful of that impact.

4. Stress.

Anxiety can be an awesome for our moods. When we are stressed, our bodies produce cortisol, which can result in greater anxiety, irritation, cravings surges and muscular tissue pains. If you feel anxiety coming on, press an anxiety sphere, walk outside, eat something, listen to music, or see an amusing clip to sidetrack on your own and alleviate the tension.

5. Enjoying The News.

While viewing the news is very important for knowing what's happening in the world and having the ability to talk openly in discussion with others, top stories on the news commonly involve political discussions, killings, fires, claims, and also other misfortunes that can be deeply distressing and can result in a darkened state of mind. After enjoying, do something more positive to get back to neutral.

6. Your Social Media Makes You Feel Inadequate.

Experts say that hanging out comparing ourselves to others, whether it be an old high school friend (or bane!) or a celeb, can make us really feel inadequate, as though our lives are much less trendy, effective or attractive as their own appear to be. Place the social media away to feel confident and a lot more in control of your life and also the fantastic things you can experience each day.

7. There's Too Much Clutter Around.

Whether there's literally way too much clutter around your house and workplace desk, or there's poor organization when it involves social and work consultations and organizing problems, excessive untidiness can make us dispirited. Check in with your room and also take into consideration whether a de-cluttering session can aid if you observe a drop in happiness and also positivity.

8. You're On A Diet.

Consuming well and living a healthy and balanced way of living is great for longterm joy and also wellness benefits; nevertheless, diets that are based on restriction and also deprivation can make us feel depressing and moody. Getting rid of all sugary foods and lures can really moisten lifestyle, so it's best to take pleasure in those in small amounts and also pursue a balance, where a lot of your meals originate from whole foods.

9. You're Out Partying All Weekend.

While being out late with friends is an enjoyable method to loosen up on the weekend break, staying out too late and drinking in unwanted can impact our state of mind overtime and make us feel short-tempered, less sad and also productive. Not only will alcohol make us psychological, however the absence of sleep will certainly add up, and it is not necessarily very easy to make up those lost hours throughout the job week.

10. You're Not Eating Enough Healthy Fats.

Healthy fats, such as unsaturated and also omega 3 fats, located in avocados, nuts, olive oil, oily fish and also coconuts, among others, can enhance levels of serotonin in the body and can add to a more favorable, peppier mood. You may experience a dulled state of mind if you are not getting sufficient of these nutrients.

11. Other People.

Professionals say that adverse state of minds can be infectious, indicating that if those around you are acting pessimistically or irritable, then you are most likely to catch on and modify your very own mood respectively. If you see someone being unfavorable around you, merely eliminate yourself from the circumstance and focus on remaining pleased and invigorated.

HOW TO RECOGNIZE AND STOP NEGATIVE EMOTIONS FROM THE MOMENT THEY HAPPEN

All of us experience feelings from an early age. As adults attempting to navigate the typically disorderly globe of modern-day life, the variety of emotions we experience in a day can change significantly.

Our capacity to respond and really feel to our feelings is typically taken for granted. We seldom stop to assume and also pay close attention to what we're really feeling. We do not consider the influence it has on our physiological and psychological states, or the long-lasting effects holding onto emotions has, that could be dangerous to us.

What are Negative Emotions?

It's vital to compare what an emotion is and what a feeling is. While both are interconnected, there's a larger distinction than you might recognize. It's certainly something that surprised me when I started with my study.

Feelings-- Emotions are considered as 'reduced level' actions. They first occur in the subcortical locations of the brain such as the amygdala and also the ventromedial prefrontal cortices. These areas are responsible for generating biochemical reactions that have a direct influence on your physical state.

Emotions are coded right into our DNA and also are believed to have created as a means to assist us react promptly to different environmental threats, much like our 'fight or trip' action. The amygdala has also been revealed to play a role in the launch of neurotransmitters that are essential for memory, which is why emotional memories are usually stronger and less complicated to recall.

Feelings have a stronger physical grounding than feelings implying researchers discover them less complicated to gauge fairly through physical cues such as blood circulation, heart rate, mind task, facial expressions, and also body language.

Sensations-- Emotions are viewed as preceding feelings, which tend to be our responses to the different feelings we experience. Where emotions can have an extra generalized experience across all human beings, sensations are a lot more subjective and are affected by our individual experiences and interpretations of our world based on those experiences.

Feelings occur in the neocortical regions of the brain and also are the next action in how we respond to our emotions as a person. Due to the fact that they are so subjective, they can not be gauged the way emotions can.

Psycho therapists have actually long checked out the variety of human feelings and their meanings. Eckman (1999) determined six first basic emotions:

Anger

Disgust

Anxiety

Happiness

Sadness

Surprise

He later expanded on this to include an additional eleven standard feelings:

Enjoyment

Ridicule

Satisfaction

Shame

Excitement

Regret

Satisfaction

Relief

Contentment

Sensory Pleasure

Embarassment

Pam (2013) specifies negative emotions "as a unhappy or unpleasant emotion which is evoked in individuals to share an unfavorable result towards an event or individual." Reading through the checklist of Eckman's standard emotions, it's fairly simple to figure out those that might be described as 'unfavorable' emotions.

While we can make use of the label unfavorable, with what we know regarding emotions, it's crucial to acknowledge that all feelings are completely typical to experience. They are a part of our embedded DNA. What is more crucial, is comprehending when and also why unfavorable feelings may arise, and establishing positive behaviors to address them.

A Look at the Psychology of Emotions

One of the a lot more popular psychological theories of feelings is Robert Plutchik's Wheel of Emotions. Plutchik (1980) mentioned that there are eight standard feelings: pleasure, depend on, concern, surprise, despair, anticipation, disgust and rage. Plutchik went better by matching the emotions with their opposites and after that producing the wheel of emotions, which offers to clarify on exactly how intricate and interactive our emotions are.

As discussed, Plutchik combined the standard emotions with their polar opposites to aid additionally establish his concept, so:

Sadness is the reverse of Joy

Anticipation is the opposite of Surprise

Temper is the reverse of Fear

Disgust is the reverse of Trust

Plutchik's wheel is a solid visual representation of exactly how our feelings present themselves. Plutchik also utilized shade to stand for the strength of the emotion: the darker the shade, the more intense it is.

It's a wonderful beginning resource for helping us even more create our understanding of just how our feelings offer themselves, exactly how they vary and just how they can connect with each various other. It has educated additionally mental research in this area and is frequently the structure where scientists checking out emotions have actually based their research study (Eckman, 1999, Parrott, 2001, Lazarus & Lazarus, 1996).

Razor et alia (1987) and later Parrott (2001) recommended a 'tree' of feelings which broke emotions right into main, secondary and also tertiary dimensions. This includes 6 key feelings (love, joy, shock, despair, concern, and rage), with linked feelings that develop at the second degree, and also again at the tertiary level. As an example, if the main feeling is delight, the second emotions can include happiness, enthrallment or optimism and the tertiary level can include pleasure, victory or hope.

Cambria, Livingstone, and also Hussain (2011) took Plutchik's wheel to an additional degree and established 'The Hourglass of Emotions'. In their publication, they improved Plutchik's eight fundamental emotions and also damaged them down into 4 measurements: sensitivity, attention, aptitude, and pleasantness. They likewise made distinctions in between which of the feelings declared (delight, expectancy, trust, and rage) or unfavorable (disgust, sadness, concern, and surprise).

Research and Studies

The more research study has actually attempted to comprehend our emotions, the a lot more that's emerged around the distinction in between negative and favorable emotions, and also the impact of each on not only our mental wellbeing but our physical wellness also.

Below I've collected a couple of summaries of the studies I found while investigating this topic that will hopefully provide you a little bit extra understanding right into our current understanding of unfavorable feelings:

Schwarz and Clore (1996) created a theory of 'feelings-as-information' which conceptualized the function of our emotions in exactly how we make judgments concerning our environment. They supposed that our emotions supply us with comments on the security of our setting and our capacity to manage provided situations. In this respect, negative emotions give us with the best indicator that something is wrong, or that our security might be compromised.

Anxiousness is typically seen as a negative emotion, however it's an essential one to stimulate us to action. We usually find it hard to react to situations without the existence of this emotion however it's essential to maintain it in check as extended anxiety can hinder our cognitive functioning (Rosen, 2008).

Adler, Rosen, and Silverstein (1998) explored the effect of negative emotions in the duty of settlement. Focusing on two negative feelings-- fear and also temper-- they located that negotiators who couldn't control or recognize these emotions when they emerged were commonly incapable to moderate the scenario successfully, despite their training. Similar study has checked out the means different feelings, such as rage and thankfulness, impact cognition and also habits within the context of arbitration (Williams and also Hinshaw, 2018).

Biswas-Diener and Kashdan (2014) wrote a whole book on the positive motivation that unfavorable emotions can relocate us towards. They see adverse feelings as motivators to help us attend to and remedy actions and also take action.

Negative emotions have likewise been researched in social contexts. Rozin et al. (1999) discovered feelings of ridicule, disgust and rage, and their effect within Japanese and american neighborhoods on values such as divinity, freedom, and area.

Assessment Theory has additionally taken a look at unfavorable emotions-- especially rage. Studies have actually found that people feel mad when they view an occasion or circumstance as personally relevant to them, inconsistent with what they are attempting to accomplish and when this is created intentionally by one more person. Appraisal philosophers highlight the role of understanding of prospective dangers

Examples of Negative Emotions

As we've begun to discover, adverse emotions are totally regular. Without them, we wouldn't have the ability to appreciate favorable ones. At the same time, if you discover you regularly tend towards one particular emotion-- specifically an unfavorable one-- it's worth checking out why that might be.

I've summed up 8 of the more typical negative feelings and why they could arise:

Anger

Exactly how does that make you feel? Your body is reacting to things not going your method, and also it's an effort to try and remedy that.

Commonly when we're upset we'll shout, our face will certainly register our temper and we may also throw things around. We're trying to get our very own method a situation and this is the only means we can believe exactly how. It's an excellent suggestion to explore why and also come up with even more favorable techniques if you're frequently reacting to situations in this means.

Nuisance

We might like our associate and love our companion these behaviors can make us feel truly annoyed. Referring to Pluchik's wheel, you can see that annoyance is the weaker form of temper. While not as intense as anger, it's the result of a similar thought procedure-- something has actually taken place or a person is doing something you wish they would not.

Fear

Fear is typically pointed out as one of the core basic feelings, and that's due to the fact that it's greatly linked with our sense of self-preservation. Accepting the emotion of concern and also discovering why it occurs can assist you prepare yourself proactively to deal with challenges.

Anxiety

Just like worry, stress and anxiety seeks to advise us regarding potential hazards and also risks. It's often seen as an unfavorable emotion as it's believed having an anxious disposition hinders judgment and our capacity to act. New research study has actually located the opposite.

Zein, Wyatt, and also Grezes (2015) discovered having stress and anxiety heightened individuals capacity to recognize faces with mad or afraid expressions. They gauged electrical signals in the mind and located that non-clinically detected participants moved their energy from sensory (expressing the emotion) to motor (physical action) circuits. Basically, individuals with anxiousness were even more ready to react and also respond to regarded risks.

Despair

When you miss a due date, obtain a bad quality, or do not secure that work you had your hopes pinned on, you'll possibly feel depressing. Despair occurs when we are dissatisfied with ourselves, our success or the behavior of somebody else around us. Despair can be good to experience as it suggests to us that we enthusiastic about something. It can be a fantastic stimulant to pursue change.

Shame

Regret is a complex feeling. We can feel this in connection with ourselves and past behaviors that we wish had not happened, however also in regard to how our actions effects those around us. Guilt is typically referred to as a 'ethical emotion' (Haidt, 2000) and can be one more solid catalyst to encourage us to make changes in our life.

Lethargy

Like sense of guilt, lethargy can be a complex emotion. If you've shed excitement, motivation or rate of interest in the important things you've previously appreciated, this might be associated with lethargy. Like anger, it can emerge when we lose control over a circumstance or scenario but instead of blowing up, we pursue a more passive-aggressive expression of rebellion.

Anguish

That's anguish and it's a feeling that arises when we aren't obtaining the outcomes we want. Misery provides us a reason to provide up on our wanted goals and it comes back to a self-preservation tactic.

What Causes Negative Emotions and Why Do We Have Them?

When you start exploring adverse emotions a little extra, you can really begin to see what might trigger or trigger them, and also why we have them in the first place.

In terms of causes, it could be a number of points:

Stress and anxiety probed going to a meeting for a new task

Anger at being caught up in traffic

Unhappiness at experiencing a split

Aggravation that a coworker hasn't done the benefit a big task

Anguish at not having the ability to stay with a brand-new workout program

Feelings give info (Schwarz and Clore, 1996) that aid you understand what is going on around you. Unfavorable emotions, in particular, can assist you acknowledge dangers (Zein, Wyatt and Grezes, 2015) and really feel prepared to favorably take care of prospective dangers (Biswas-Diener and also Kashdan, 2014).

Various experiences in our lives will certainly provoke different psychological responses, to differing degrees of strength. As a person, you will certainly experience a complete variety of emotions throughout your lifetime in response to swiftly transforming situations.

Do We Want to Overcome and Stop Negative Emotions Altogether?

Essentially, no.

It's regular for us to want to move far from feelings that make us really feel negative. As a transformative action, unfavorable feelings in the modern globe are not really a sign of an extreme threat against us, however overcoming and quiting them completely would be hugely harmful to us.

Unfavorable emotions are an exceptionally typical, healthy and also useful part of life. I think it's really vital not to fall into the 'happiness catch' of thinking that these emotions signify weak point or low psychological knowledge. I understand from individual experience that trying to hide away from negative feelings, can cause further emotional discomfort.

As a human being, you will certainly experience a complete variety of emotions throughout your lifetime in action to swiftly transforming situations. No emotion lacks purpose. It's when we start to further understand the purpose and also discover behind each emotion, that we find out new means to respond which sustains our emotional development and also sense of wellness.

When exploring negative feelings, it's additionally important to know that they are not the only resource of information you have access to. Prior to you act on any type of feeling you need to likewise seek to explore your previous experiences, kept knowledge and memories, personal values and desired outcomes for any provided circumstance (Shpancer, 2010). Remember-- feelings are a low-level reaction so you reach determine exactly how you react to them and also not allow them pirate your actions.

What are the Effects of Negative Emotions?

While understanding that adverse emotions are a healthy part of life is important, there is a disadvantage to providing too much cost-free regime.

If you invest way too much time residence on unfavorable feelings and also the scenarios that might have triggered them, you might go into a spiral of rumination. Rumination is the tendency to maintain thinking, repeating, or obsessing over negative psychological circumstances and experiences (Nolen-Hoeksema, 1991). In this spiral of negative thinking, you can wind up feeling even worse and even worse concerning the circumstance and yourself, the result of which could be a variety of damaging effects to your physical and psychological well-being.

The problem with rumination is that it increases your brain's stress and anxiety reaction circuit, implying your body obtains unnecessarily flooded with the stress hormone cortisol. There's substantial proof that this is a driver for clinical depression (Izard, 2009).

Further research has actually connected the tendency to ponder to a number of dangerous coping behaviors, such as alcohol, overindulging and also smoking cigarettes consumption, together with physical wellness repercussions including insomnia, hypertension, heart disease, and scientific anxiety and clinical depression (Gerin et al, 2012, Dimsdale, 2008, Everson et alia, 1998).

Another research located that people who delighted in prolonged rumination after a negative emotional experience took longer to recover from the physiological impact of the experience (Szabo et al, 2017).

Rumination can be a difficult technicality to leave, especially as most people don't realize they're embeded pondering rut and also instead believe they are proactively issue fixing (Yapko, 2015). This can result in more effects for physical and psychological wellbeing.

How Can They Impact our Health and Well-Being?

It's not adverse emotions that straight affect our health and wellness and wellness, but just how we react and process them when we do experience them that really counts.

Remaining stuck on negative emotions can boost our bodies' production of our stress hormonal agent, cortisol, which in turn depletes our cognitive capacity to trouble address proactively and can additionally damage our immune defenses, making us extra at risk to various other ailment (Iliard, 2009). Chronic tension has actually also been connected to a shorter life-span (Epel et al, 2004).

Temper is the unfavorable emotion that has been shown to have the largest influence on our health and also health, especially where this is poorly taken care of. Research studies have actually connected temper to numerous health issues including high blood pressure, heart disease and also digestive conditions (Hendricks et alia, 2013).

Boerma (2007) linked harmful amounts of anger to increased levels of cortisol, which were implicated in lowered body immune system effectiveness. Boerma's research study found that constantly upset individuals were more probable to have a cold, the influenza, asthmatic signs and symptoms and also skin illness such as rashes compared to non-chronically mad individuals.

A more recent location of study has discovered the influence of unfavorable feelings on our sensory understandings and experiences. Kelley and also Schmeichel (2014) explored the influence of worry and anger on our feeling of touch. Individuals were asked to remember, relive and also compose up a personal experience that evoked a concern reaction or an angry action.

The scientists then carried out a two-point discrimination procedure-- generally, the individual's hand was concealed from their view and also they were poked in their index finger with either one factor or more points.

Participants after that had to determine whether they were poked by a couple of instruments. Higher error recommends a diminished sense of touch. When identifying in between one or two points of get in touch with, individuals that were asked to recall a fear feedback consistently showed a decreased sense of touch.

The study into the influence of adverse emotions on our sensory assumptions is still emerging, but it could provide some fantastic insights right into why we could hold on to adverse emotions and also how they influence our memory of unfavorable scenarios.

Negative Emotions and Cancer

Some research has actually started to check out the web link in between adverse feelings and also cancer. Once again, in this area, most of the study has concentrated specifically on anger as a negative emotion and its web link to cancer.

Anger as a feeling is normal to really feel, yet as we've currently seen from the research study, it's exactly how it's expressed-- or otherwise revealed-- that can create issues. When temper is extended and intense, or on the flip side, quelched, it becomes what scientists describe as unhealthy anger (Enright & Fitzgibbons, 2015).

Undesirable temper in its quelched state has actually been connected to cancer cells. Thomas at al (2000) found that patients with cancer likewise provided exceptionally reduced temper scores when checked, which they really felt recommended that the clients were repressing or subduing their rage. The scientists recommended that this was evidence that quelched temper might be a forerunner to the advancement of cancer.

Various other study appears to sustain their claim. In studies with women diagnosed with breast cancer, scientists report a statistically considerable partnership in between what they refer to as extreme suppression of temper, and also the medical diagnosis of bust cancer cells (Greer and Morris, 1975). Ladies who quelched their temper showed increased degrees of lotion Immunoglobulin A, which has actually been connected to some autoimmune illness (Pettingale, Greer and Tee, 1977).

Penedo et al (2006) focused on the effect of quelched temper in connection to prostate cancer cells. They discovered a strong presence of the Natural Killer Cell Cytotoxicity in guys who reported that they really did not repress their rage.

It additionally doesn't reveal a strong link between temper and all cancers, only selective ones. What these researches do offer is an understanding right into the long-lasting impacts of unfavorable emotions like anger when they are not managed in positive methods.

Exactly How Can We Best Control and Deal with our Negative Emotions?

Among the most effective ways to take care of our negative emotions is via acceptance.

Just as there are benefits to negative emotions, requiring ourselves to be pleased constantly can additionally be harmful to our total psychological health.

Approving adverse feelings, in ourselves and others, are all a component of being human allows us to build far better empathy for just how they might offer themselves and why. Rather than coming to be stuck in a mindset that negative feelings require to be stayed clear of or that they are in some way 'incorrect' to experience, we need to approve they are an all-natural part of that we are.

When we do that we can actually start to change exactly how we may respond to them and develop actions that are purposeful and also bring value to exactly how we reveal ourselves and involve with others.

6 Tips to Manage, Process and Embrace Negative Emotions

As positive psychology has gotten more understanding right into our negative feelings, it's also had the ability to supply us with numerous strategies for balancing these emotions within our everyday lives.

Sims (2017) discovered methods to proactively refine and acknowledge negative feelings and created the phrase TEARS of HOPE to help trainer and guide people. Right here's what it stands for:

T = Teach and Learn

This is the process of paying attention to what your body is attempting to show you through the presentation of adverse feelings, and discover what they mean. It's building your own personal knowledge of the method you respond to emotional states, interpreting the signals your body is sending you, and acknowledging that they serve a function.

E = Express and also enable

Negative feelings motivate us to reveal them. They are very workable emotions. The express and also allow part of the phrase motivates you to explore this with openness and also inquisitiveness. It's about enhancing your acceptance of your natural reactions and enabling them to be present without resentment.

A= Accept and also befriend

This complies with on nicely from express and also enable. It's about befriending yourself and also the way you are as a human. Focus on boosting your acceptance with favorable affirmations to bring your round of unfavorable emotions right into a space of acceptance.

R = Re-appraise and re-frame

You can start to focus on reframing the situation and how you react when you've started to accept that this is an all-natural part of that you are. Even if an adverse emotion has occurred, does not imply you have to respond in manner ins which are damaging to you and also those around you.

Approving negative emotions isn't regarding approving or excusing poor habits, it's regarding creating awareness for the self and also others to produce positive reactions.

S = Social support

Knowing that adverse feelings exist in all of us, and also in practically the same way, can be a superb source of compassion and empathy to those around us. It's exactly how we refine our feelings that differ, so seeing somebody in the tosses of anger, recognizing that they are just managing a viewed danger can actually urge us to approach them with compassion, instead of temper ourselves.

H = Hedonic health and happiness

This is the procedure of grouping positive experiences with negative. It can be beneficial for us to organize them with positive experiences so we don't fall right into a ruminating trap because we more conveniently recall negative experiences. This way, we can focus more of our energy on recalling the favorable experiences.

O = Observe and also participate in

Take the time to truly observe your responses without ignoring them, quelching them, or over overemphasizing them. Use mindfulness to bring your emphasis to your body and mind and what a specific feeling is developing within you. Take care of these responses without judgment.

P = Physiology and also behavior modifications

Equally as you observe your psychological and emotional reactions, observe your physical reactions also. Bring your focus to your breath, your heart price and also feeling out the modifications in your physiology that an unfavorable emotion may have triggered. Again, take care of these modifications without judgment.

E = Eudaimonia

This might not be a word you are familiar with, however it's well worth contributing to your vocabulary. Eudaimonia is a Greek word which primarily describes having a good spirit. It suggests you have located a state of being that mores than happy, flourishing and also healthy, and you have found out to take part in actions that lead to your overall wellness. It suggests you're actively aiming in the direction of a feeling of authenticity in all you do.

I've undergone the research readily available and additionally looked at the listed below ideas to aid you take care of, process and also welcome adverse feelings in manner ins which will certainly aid you to find and comprehend value in them:

Envisage your 'Best Possible Self'

If you feel like your negative emotions are obtaining the most effective of you, that you're not sharing them in healthy and balanced methods or obtaining embeded pondering habits, a simple visualization strategy could assist.

As opposed to concentrating just on the negative feeling or what you're doing incorrect, concentrate rather on what you would certainly like the behavior to be.

What does the ideal feasible version of you look like in that circumstance? Exactly how would they react? You can do this as a psychological visual workout or a journal workout.

Putting in the time as soon as a week to exercise this can have remarkable outcomes on not just your mood however just how you approach the scenario following time it happens.

Practice Gratitude

Practicing gratefulness has actually been shown to have remarkable results for both the receivers and givers. These impacts have long getting to impacts on our mood and assumption of occasions, so it's worth investing a little bit of time adding the method to your weekly collection.

Whether it's for a huge point or a little point, personally, over the phone, a letter or an easy text, letting somebody know you value them or something they have done, can really make a distinction in exactly how you perceive and respond to unfavorable emotions.

Explore mindfulness methods

If you find you have a short fuse and anger is your go-to negative emotion (or if you discover you're constantly on the range of the temper emotion, regularly experiencing inconvenience) mindfulness could assist to reframe what you're really feeling.

Follow the TEARS of HOPE advice and also put in the time to recognize why you may be reacting this way. Mindfulness can aid you find the headspace to do this in a favorable way.

Discover how to respond versus respond

Do you know the distinction in between just how you respond versus exactly how you respond? Adverse emotions often encourage us to respond quickly to an offered situation. We might lash out or shout when we feel angry. We might withdraw and reject individuals around us when we become depressing.

Occasionally we require to act upon these impulses, yet primarily we do not. By discovering your negative emotions you can start to establish your understanding of how you react, and also instead begin to switch this to favorable means of reacting-- which might imply learning that no response is required in any way.

When to take a break, Know

Know when to take a day to yourself. If you are continuously battling and experiencing adverse feelings to handle them, your body is informing you something isn't.

Take a day to re-center. Load this particular day with positive experiences, doing the important things that you know gas you and make you really feel great. This type of break can assist to realign your thinking, provide you some room to refocus on why you may be experiencing the adverse feelings, and come up with some favorable coping techniques.

This is simply a fast relation of the pointers I felt would be most useful, yet everything comes down to you as an individual. Some of them might function really well, and others not a lot. See to it you check out a couple of different strategies and also find the ones that function best for you.

A Look at Negative Emotions in the Workplace

Our work and the work environment can be sources of fantastic joy and also accomplishment for us. On the flip side, they can also be a battlefield for dissatisfaction and a range of negative emotions. These feelings can be doubly bothering at the workplace as we attempt to handle our reactions before expert colleagues and our boss. Falling short to do so can cause our task getting on the line. I'm pretty sure that's something all of us want to avoid!

Listed below I've taken 5 of the most typical unfavorable emotions that emerge at work and also what they may be signaling:

Anger-- Anger at the office can occur for a number of different reasons. You could be discouraged with a slack coworker, a tyrannical manager, lessenings or unfair treatment.

Of all the negative feelings, temper is possibly the one you most intend to maintain in check in the workplace. If you really feel the experience of anger climbing at work, bear in mind to respond and also not react.

Remove on your own from the scenario by walking and getting some fresh air. Use mindfulness to bring your mind and body back to a state of calm and approach the problem reasonably.

Or you may feel worry and anxiety since of a harmful employer or coworker. Your worry is informing you that you don't feel risk-free.

If you're stressed over task security, ensuring you upgrade your Curriculum Vitae and taking a course to upgrade your abilities, can make you feel positive and in control of your scenario. Look for assistance when it comes to a hazardous colleague or employer. Talk with a trusted colleague, pal or HR representative and get advice.

Regret-- Guilt is a challenging one. Maybe you took a sick day when you should not have actually or condemned an associate when you missed out on a target date. Shame is your ethical compass informing you something is awry. When the feeling arises and seek to make adjustments, you can't go back and also alter previous behaviors yet you can pay interest.

Jealousy-- Is there one particular associate who constantly seems to get the praise? That may have pipped you for that promo, pay increase or large customer? Jealousy can emerge at the workplace when we really feel somebody is achieving the goals we want to accomplish ourselves however may be having difficulty in doing so.

Instead of ending up being bitter, come close to the associate for advice on exactly how you might be able to boost also. Seek their help and you might create an alliance that enjoys benefits, rather of a feud that profits no one.

Passiveness-- Feeling indifferent in your work duty or tasks is a sign that this requires to be discovered. It might be a sign that it's time to move on or seek new difficulties if you're feeling disengaged from your work and coworkers.

Nobody likes being burnt out and this could be your passive-aggressive way of sticking your heels in instead of accepting change as required. If this feeling of passiveness is spreading right into other areas of your life, maybe a sign of anxiety, so make sure to look for specialist assistance if you're discovering it difficult to feel determined concerning life.

Just as unfavorable emotions beyond work are an indication that something needs to change, the same is true when they take place at the workplace. Check out the feeling proactively and see where it leads you.

RECOGNIZE WHAT CAUSES YOUR MOOD SWINGS

When you're satisfied, it's normal to have days where you really feel depressing or days. As long as your mood changes do not interfere with your life to a severe degree, they're usually considered to be healthy and balanced.

On the other hand, you may have a medical condition if you change from extremely happy to extremely dispirited regularly. If you have regular and also serious changes in state of mind, you need to tell your doctor regarding them. They can go over the possible reasons for why you're experiencing them.

Some causes of fast adjustments in actions can be connected to mental health and wellness, hormonal agents, material use, or various other health and wellness problems.

" Mood swings" is an usual term made use of to explain extremely fluctuating and also quick feelings. People typically explain state of mind swings as a "roller rollercoaster" of sensations from happiness and also contentment to temper, impatience, and even anxiety.1.

A person may identify something that has actually "triggered" a change in their mood, such as a demanding occasion at the workplace. It's also not unusual for state of mind swings to occur without an evident cause. Individuals might experience these adjustments in state of mind throughout a day or perhaps within a couple of hrs.

For example, your irritated colleague might say they "woke up on the incorrect side of the bed" when they arrive at the office feeling short-tempered. Their state of mind might have enhanced when you see them later on in the day. They may not also remember why they were in a poor mood before.

Possibly your associate simply isn't much of a morning person, yet their mood normally raises as they get up and they feel much more ready for the day in advance. The body's circadian rhythm, which is understood for affecting when we sleep, likewise drives our mood throughout the day to a specific extent.

If you observe your discontented coworker has more springtime in their action after they have breakfast and a mug of coffee, their poor early morning mood may have been stemming from caffeine withdrawal or reduced blood sugar (hypoglycemia).

Causes.

Everyone experiences state of mind swings periodically, however if you appear to get them regularly or they are so extreme that they disrupt your day-to-day live (consisting of work and relationships), it might suggest an underlying condition that needs treatment.

Illness and Injury.

Despite the fact that the term "state of mind swings" suggests an emotional origin, the shifts can likewise be related to persistent illness or acute injuries that affect the mind, such as dementia, concussion, or a stroke.

Various other clinical problems (particularly neurological conditions) can additionally create mood swings, including:.

Diabetic issues.

Rest disorders.

Several sclerosis.

Thyroid disorders.

Parkinson's condition.

Developmental.

Toddlers and young children typically appear "moody" and might throw outbursts as they learn to regulate their emotions. While they're typically a normal component of psychological development, mood swings in kids can additionally signify an underlying psychological health and wellness disorder, finding out impairment, and even a physical condition.

Kids and teenagers with interest deficiency hyperactivity problem (ADHD) might experience changes in mood that can conflict with school and relationships.

As youngsters grow older, mood swings continue to be a typical part of their development. By the time they get in the preteen years, changes in mood are largely driven by hormone adjustments. These changes in mood tend to peak during adolescence and also gradually maintain by young their adult years.

Internal adjustments that take place throughout our lives influence our state of mind, but it's not simply what's happening inside that determines how we feel; we also reply to what's occurring around us. Outside modifications to our lives and in our environments, such as boosted stress at institution, work, or home, can likewise influence our feelings.8.

Diet regimen.

An individual who is eating a diet plan that's nutritionally poor or otherwise getting enough to consume might experience state of mind modifications in reaction to changing blood sugar levels and also malnourishment.

Digestive conditions that affect the body's ability to soak up nutrients, such as Celiac illness and inflammatory bowel illness (IBD), have actually been connected with mood swings. These problems have also be linked to certain psychological health conditions, such as clinical depression.9.

Allergic reactions.

You might find that your mood is influenced by the time of year you often tend to have symptoms if you have seasonal allergic reactions. Consistent sneezing, watery eyes, and irritation can likewise cause fatigue, particularly if they interfere with rest.

Rest.

An individual's state of mind can additionally be heavily influenced by the quantity and quality of rest they get. A person who is sleep-deprived (specifically when persistent) may experience intense mood changes along with various other psychological signs.

Medicines and Substance Use.

Stopping a prescription or beginning drug can likewise affect an individual's state of mind. While medicines such as antidepressants and mood stabilizers are expected to transform a person's moods, medicines prescribed for various other reasons may additionally cause state of mind swings as a side effect.

For instance, people that take anabolic steroids can experience intense state of mind adjustments-- even craze. If a person (such as a professional athlete) misuses steroid medications, symptoms might be also life-threatening and erratic.

People that are handling material usage conditions may also be extra prone to experiencing severe changes in state of mind, particularly when they are incapable to make use of a substance or get, or when they are trying to quit a drug (withdrawal).

Even though state of mind changes can be a symptom of depression or an additional psychological health and wellness condition, some medications utilized to deal with these disorders can also trigger modifications in state of mind. In some cases, these state of mind changes show that the medication isn't the right option for treatment, or that the medical diagnosis someone has actually been provided may not be appropriate.

As an example, a person that has bipolar affective disorder may be misdiagnosed with clinical depression and suggested medication. Specific antidepressants may cause a manic episode in someone with bipolar condition.

If state of mind swings begin unexpectedly, are extremely unreasonable, or come to be suicidal, look for immediate treatment.

Hormonal agents.

Various other feasible causes of mood swings may come from a discrepancy of the mind chemicals that are associated with mood law, as when it comes to bipolar affective disorder.

Fluctuations in mind chemicals can additionally be a typical feature, such as the hormonal modifications of the menstrual cycle. For the very same reason, state of mind swings are likewise usual in feedback to other causes of shifting levels of hormones (particularly estrogen), such as pregnancy and menopause.

A person's danger for anxiety is boosted during these times as well, so state of mind swings can additionally be an indicator of a mental health problem.

Certain forms of hormone birth control, such as the Pill, may assist reduce mood swings related to the menstruation, yet it's likewise been recommended that adjustments in state of mind might be a side effect of these drugs.

However, even more study is needed, as other researches did not discover a web link in between contraceptive pills and also mood swings.

Mood Swings & Mental Illness.

While shifts in mood can be completely normal, set off by stress and anxiety, and/or component of managing a physical health and wellness condition, state of mind swings can also be a signs and symptom of mental disease.

When characterizing and also detecting psychological health conditions (specifically bipolar illness and also borderline character problem) the constellation of intense, rapid, and regular changes in state of mind is sometimes referred to as "psychological lability." 15.

However, a labile mood is not unique to mental disease. It's likewise seen in individuals with stressful mind injury, stroke, and also Alzheimer's, along with various other medical conditions.

If you are experiencing changes in mood along with other particular symptoms and signs of a psychological health condition, talk with your medical professional. Comprehending the underlying reason is essential to finding the most reliable means to handle mood swings.

Depression

If it is without treatment), state of mind swings are likewise usual with clinical depression (particularly. An individual's state of mind may change from irritation to extreme despair to an upset outburst.16.

Individuals who are dispirited may additionally have other signs, such as:.

Really feeling unfortunate, helpless, and useless.

Have problem resting or resting way too much.

Consuming more than usual or otherwise eating enough.

Really feeling exhausted, tired, and fatigued.

No more enjoying favorite activities.

Difficulty focusing and/or choosing.

Having thoughts of fatality or self-destruction.

Comparable to clinical depression and also in some cases considered a "milder" form of bipolar illness, cyclothymia is a problem defined by periods of reduced state of mind that alternate with hypomania.

Bipolar illness.

State of mind swings are a hallmark sign of bipolar problem. There are 2 primary types of bipolar condition: Bipolar I and also Bipolar II.

The swings state of mind for individuals with bipolar disorder may consist of some or all of the signs of a manic/hypomanic or depressive episode.

An individual experiencing an episode of mania might:.

Talk a lot/very fast.

Have excess power.

Engage in high-risk habits.

Appear "on side" or short-tempered.

Feel like sleeping much less than they typically do (yet do not really feel the need for even more sleep).

Be a lot more ambitious or energetic than common (e.g. handling brand-new tasks, functioning more/harder, starting brand-new hobbies).

Throughout a duration of anxiety, a person may:.

Feel worthless or helpless.

Seem depressing, cry often, or be tearful.

Have no power, feel exhausted or "wiped out".

Seem like they can not focus or concentrate or thoughts/tasks.

Stop sensation like doing things they made use of to enjoy (ex-spouse. hobbies).

Rest more than usual OR be not able to fall/stay asleep.

Consume more or less than they normally do (weight-loss or gain).

Have thoughts of dying or death; planning/attempting self-destruction.

How long it takes for the episodes to change an individual's mood to change to the other end of the spectrum can differ from one person to another. People who have "rapid-cycling" signs might experience changes weekly or daily, while others may remain in one sort of episode for months or years.

Drugs used to deal with bipolar illness might assist handle these intense shifts. Of note, researchers are getting better at anticipating the state of mind changes in people with bipolar affective disorder, which might help physicians identify and deal with the condition.

Borderline Personality Disorder.

Borderline personality problem (BPD) is an additional mental health and wellness condition that can cause relentless mood swings. These state of mind changes are normally intense and variable and can last from a few hours to a couple of days.

Various other signs of BPD include:.

Risky and impulsive habits (vulnerable sex, reckless driving, substance abuse).

Severe reactions (rage, panic) to desertion (real or envisioned).

Feeling restless or empty.

Self-harming, threatening or trying self-destruction.

Emotional and intense relationships with others.

Rage concerns (outbursts, inappropriate rage, inability to manage temper).

Dissociative signs (loss of time, really feeling "outdoors" one's very own body).

Coping

Mood swings can be testing to deal with, particularly if they interfere with your day-to-day life, school or job, and your relationships.

Changes in state of mind that are regular and extreme must be discussed with your physician, as you will need to figure out the underlying clinical and/or mental health and wellness cause before you can successfully treat them.

Drugs called state of mind stabilizers, psychotherapy or counseling, and treatments such as cognitive-behavioral treatment (CBT) may be helpful if an underlying mental disease is creating state of mind swings or making them worse.

You might have the ability to manage less frequent, light, or periodic mood swings by yourself, particularly if you have a common sense of what "triggers" them. The initial step is recognizing factors in your life and atmosphere, such as tension, inadequate rest, or missing your morning coffee, that can trigger state of mind swings.

To better deal and also handle with these adjustments in mood, you might intend to try out different strategies, such as:

Getting regular exercise

Workout can be a great way to raise your mood and boost your ability to take care of stress. When you work out, your body commonly really feels more unwinded and also tranquil, yet there are mental benefits, as well. Learn why exercise is helpful, and which kinds of workouts are best to help stabilize your feelings.

Exactly How Exercise Improves Mood

When you take part in high-intensity exercise, your body and brain produce hormonal agents, and also natural chemicals that have a positive influence on your mood, memory, power levels, and also sense of wellness. Some of these are known as endorphins, the body's feel-good chemicals. They can cause the "runner's high" that joggers discuss.

After a good exercise, your muscle mass are tired, but you really feel more unwinded. You might likewise really feel a feeling of achievement, which improves your self-confidence and enhances your sense of wellness. Thanks to your exercise, the pent-up stress and stress and anxiety in your muscle mass and your mind are reduced.

Workout and Emotions

While exercise is not, on its own, a treatment for depression, studies reveal that even a single round of workout leads to positive modifications in brain chemicals and can boost your state of mind. A 2017 review on the results of exercise released in the journal Brain Plasticity, located that after workout, people reported a much better mood with decreases in stress, temper, and also anxiety.

In fact, for people with moderate or light clinical depression, 30 mins of intense workout might be effective for boosting state of mind. A testimonial study that considered 23 randomized controlled researches discovered integrating exercise with traditional medication and cognitive behavior modification treatment for clinical depression reduced clinical depression signs and symptoms even more.

A lot of research studies on exercise and also mood show that 30 mins of everyday workout is enough to reap the benefits. A lot more exercise isn't necessarily going to make you better, and also as with anything, it's feasible to exaggerate it. For example, among the advantages of exercise is that it promotes cortisol manufacturing, which can aid with memory and also performance. On the various other hand, way too much cortisol can have negative results on your body and also for your state of mind.

Sorts of Exercises to Improve Mood

It's critical that you select something you take pleasure in when it comes to exercise. Cardiovascular exercise is wonderful, but if you hate running or swimming, you will not stay with it. and when an activity is more enjoyable, chances are much better for lasting adherence.

For your exercise regimen, you may attempt a mix of singular activities like walking, swimming, or gardening, incorporated with some team activities like high-intensity period training classes or regular team walkings or bike flights. In addition to the endorphin and also physical benefits of workout, an additional possible benefit of exercise is the possibility for social interaction, which can usually improve your state of mind just as much.

The very best kind of workout to improve your state of mind is commonly a mix of tasks you enjoy and also are encouraged to stick with for the long term.

For mood-lifting benefits, try any type of or all of the following tasks. Some people obtain burnt out with the very same workout every day; others enjoy the regimen. Consider keeping the exercises you like as your anchor exercises, and after that regularly exchanging in various other activities as your climate, routine, or state of mind modifications. For group courses, maintain your eye open for seasonal discount rates or Groupon deals.

Cardiovascular and Aerobic Exercises

Cardiovascular and also cardio workouts are terrific for producing the strength required for the launch of mood-raising endorphins in your body. Cardiovascular exercises are those that get your heart price up, like jogging, swimming, biking, vigorous walking, or utilizing an elliptical fitness instructor. You can also get your heart price up by doing tasks like horticulture and dance-- both have actually been revealed to minimize depression and anxiousness.

Joining a local league to play basketball, football, or tennis can supply social interaction while providing you a cardio workout if you such as sporting activities. Signing up with a group course that provides a high-intensity interval exercise like Crossfit or boxing is another means to get your cardio in while having some fun with friends.

Yoga

Yoga is a system of all natural health and also spiritual growth which focuses on reflection, breathing exercises, and also physical positions. Unless you're doing an energetic flow or vinyasa yoga exercise course, yoga doesn't provide much of a cardio workout. It can, nevertheless, educate you how to unwind, release stress, stretch tight muscle mass, and also even enhance weak ones. Doing yoga exercise frequently can aid to ease anxiety and enhance feelings of well-being. A 2016 testimonial write-up on the use of yoga for anxiety and clinical depression located that the practice is beneficial for minimizing anxiousness, depression, and signs related to post-traumatic stress disorder (PTSD).

Tai Chi

A typical Chinese exercise that is practiced worldwide, tai chi can benefit individuals that experience signs and symptoms of anxiety and depression, and also it has actually been revealed to enhance immune function along with to boost the blood degrees of feel-good endorphins.

Any person can do tai chi due to the fact that the movements are quickly discovered and repetitive. According to conventional Chinese medicine, the method assists to relieve power blockages in the body, which aids to protect against or deal with particular diseases. Studies recommend that tai chi can enhance many elements of health including decreasing anxiety, stress and anxiety, stress and anxiety.

Making changes to your diet

There are numerous foods that have been connected to mood, including those that are helpful in the therapy prepares for those with anxiety. While foods might not be the magic bullet for illness, such as depression or other mental ailments, there is sufficient proof to show a link between diet and mood.

The Link Between Food and also Mood

There are unlimited situations in which the link between food and also state of mind can be seen. Some might say, that food has a sugar pill effect, but proof sustains the reality that food can play a function in exactly how our brain responds.

The foods that comprise our diet plan have actually been revealed to have an effect in our brain from both a chemical and physiologic viewpoint. and it is these changes that can bring about differences in exactly how we feel and how we act.

Depression, which afflicts over 19 million Americans, results from a chemical discrepancy so possibly an adjustment in diet is in order. Autism has been linked to research studies on mind function and brain chemistry, so it is no surprise that many therapy plans consist of changes in diet plan. There are numerous various other problems for which modifying the diet plan is amongst the referrals.

Taking it one action even more, exactly how regarding the mind chemistry for someone with a food allergic reaction? Is there a link to state of mind also?

Numerous researches reveal that amongst the signs and symptoms of itchy throats, hives, stomach aches, and also migraines, are records of the so-called "brain fog" and mood-related concerns that go along with food allergies.

In the case of a food allergy, your body declines the food and starts to eliminate it off, as if it is a foreign body. This reaction can then straight impact the body's brain chemistry and production of neurotransmitters and hormones. In instances of food allergies and intolerances, there is proof of state of mind modifications and also state of mind swings.

Celiac patients have long reported "brain haze" when they have mistakenly eaten gluten. Temper and also impatience is frequently seen in children who have a dairy products allergic reaction. Numerous countries have even prohibited using food additive in foods, as it has actually had harmful behavioral effects on youngsters.

For those with food allergic reactions, it is likewise crucial to not only check out the symptoms of the allergic reaction yet to look at the total diet plan intake. As soon as a food or food team is gotten of the diet plan, there is a chance that it is the deficiency that is currently triggering a disruption to their mood.

The brain is our most complex organ doing one of the most function. It must be working at perpetuity, even when you are asleep. Consequently, what you consume has a direct impact on your brain function and behavior, namely state of mind.

Serotonin is the neurotransmitter that is in charge of managing points like cravings, mood, rest and regulating pain. With nearly all of your body's serotonin being produced in your stomach system, it is not surprising that your diet plan plays a critical role in its production.

Adenosine is another neurotransmitter discovered in the mind that can work as an all-natural downer. High levels of caffeine, on the other hand, has been linked to blocking, adenosine manufacturing, a chemical that can protect against brain-boosting energy, making depression even worse. Yet, one more way in which food and state of mind have actually been connected.

Foods to Boost Mood

What does one consume to be and also maintain a healthy and balanced diet plan in a good mood? There are several food options to improve general health. It is just as important to maintain in foods that can spruce up your state of mind. And for those with food allergies, it is a lot more crucial to take a more detailed look at what you can contribute to improve your diet plan and also keep you happier.

Maybe beginning with these straightforward food suggestions can set you on your means to a larger smile.

Bananas

This fruit is both abundant and nourishing in tryptophan, which is the chemical that is converted into serotonin. Most importantly the tryptophan converts to serotonin as quickly as the banana is taken in, leaving you feeling happy and unwinded in no time in any way.

Salmon

This fish is rich in omega-3 fatty acids, especially one called EPA. This omega-3 fatty acid has been shown to boost your brain and convenience anxiety.

Dark Chocolate

Eating this treat can absolutely lift your state of mind. This food boosts the production of endorphins, which are the mind chemicals that prompt sensations of enjoyment.

Blueberries and Blackberries

Both of these berries are rich in antioxidants, which serve to assist your mind in the manufacturing of a chemical called dopamine. Dopamine plays a critical role in memory and state of mind.

Eggs

A terrific high biological worth healthy protein helps to keep your blood glucose also, to aid maintain a positive mood.

Greek Yogurt

This calcium-rich food is sure to assist raise your mood. When your body has the right amount of calcium degrees, it sends out a signal for your body to release neurotransmitters that make you really feel excellent. Without ideal degrees of calcium, frequently anxiety and anxiousness can be exacerbated.

Following time you order a treat and want to place on a happy face, think about what foods may really uplift your mood.

LEARNING STRESS MANAGEMENT
TECHNIQUES

Most of us experience stress and anxiety in our lives. Because the large bulk of health issue are created or influenced by tension, it is very important to comprehend how tension influences your body and discover efficient anxiety administration techniques to make stress and anxiety help you instead of versus you.

What Is Stress?

Stress is your body's reaction to modifications in your life. Due to the fact that life entails continuous change (ranging from transforming areas from house to function each morning to adapting to major life modifications like marriage, divorce, or fatality of a liked one), there is no avoiding anxiety.1 This is why your goal should not be to remove all stress and anxiety but to eliminate unnecessary stress and properly manage the rest. There are some usual causes of stress and anxiety that many individuals experience, yet each person is various.

Root causes of Stress

Anxiety can come from several resources, which are called "stress factors." Because our experience of what is considered "stressful" is developed by our special understandings of what we experience in life (based upon our own mix of characteristic, available sources, regular idea patterns), a scenario may be perceived as "stressful" by one person and also merely "difficult" by another person.

Put simply, a single person's tension trigger might not sign up as difficult to somebody else. That said, particular scenarios often tend to trigger more anxiety in many people and can enhance the threat of burnout. As an example, when we find ourselves in circumstances where there are high needs on us; where we have little control and couple of choices; where we do not really feel geared up; where we may be roughly evaluated by others; and where effects for failure are unforeseeable or steep, we often tend to get stressed out.

Because of this, many people are worried by their jobs, their connections, their financial issues, illness, and more ordinary points like clutter or busy routines. Discovering abilities to handle these stressors can help reduce your experience of stress and anxiety.1.

Impacts of Stress.

Just as stress and anxiety is regarded differently by each of us, stress and anxiety affects us all in manner ins which are unique to us.

A single person might experience headaches, while another may find indigestion is a typical reaction, and also a 3rd may experience any of a number of other signs. While most of us react to stress and anxiety in our own methods, there is a lengthy listing of frequently seasoned impacts of anxiety that variety from mild to dangerous. Stress can influence resistance, which can impact essentially all areas of health and wellness. Stress can impact mood in several methods too.

Talk to your doctor to be sure you are doing what you can to guard your health if you locate yourself experiencing physical symptoms you assume might be connected to stress. Signs and symptoms that may be aggravated by tension are not "all in your head" and also need to be taken seriously.

Reliable Stress Management.

Tension can be effectively handled in many different means. The very best stress and anxiety monitoring plans normally include a mix of tension relievers that resolve anxiety literally and also emotionally and also aid to create resilience and coping skills.

7 Highly Effective Stress Relievers.

Usage quick stress reducers. Some stress relief methods can work in simply a few minutes to calm the body's stress and anxiety action. These techniques provide a "quick solution" that assists you really feel calmer right now, and this can aid in numerous means. When your anxiety feedback is not triggered, you might approach troubles more thoughtfully and proactively. You might be less likely to lash out at others out of aggravation, which can maintain your relationships healthier. Nipping your stress and anxiety feedback in the bud can also keep you from experiencing persistent stress.

Quick stress relievers like breathing exercises, as an example, might not construct your durability to future anxiety or minimize the stress factors that you face, yet they can help soothe the body's physiology once the stress and anxiety action is caused.

Create stress-relieving routines. Some methods are less practical to use when you remain in the middle of a difficult situation. If you exercise them on a regular basis, they can assist you manage stress and anxiety in basic by being less responsive to it and also a lot more able to reverse your anxiety reaction swiftly and easily.

Long-lasting healthy and balanced habits, like workout or regular meditation, can assist to promote resilience toward stress factors if you make them a regular component of your life.3 Communication skills and other way of living abilities can be helpful in taking care of stressors and also changing just how we really feel from "overwhelmed" to "challenged" or perhaps "promoted.".

You may not be able to completely remove stress from your life or also the biggest stress factors, but there are locations where you can minimize it and get it to a manageable level. Any type of stress that you can reduce out can reduce your total anxiety lots.

Finding a wide variety of stress management strategies, and after that choosing a mix that fits your needs, can be a key technique for reliable tension alleviation.

Is Stress Inevitably Harmful to Health?

Actually, no. There are a number of various sorts of tension that variety from eustress, which is a positive and exciting type of stress and anxiety, to chronic tension, which has been connected to numerous major health issues and also is the sort of unfavorable tension frequently discussed current.1 While we want to take care of or remove the negative kinds of stress, we likewise want to keep positive types of stress and anxiety in our lives to help us stay essential and also to life. Nevertheless, if we experience too much tension in our lives, also "good" stress and anxiety can add to excessive stress and anxiety levels, which can result in sensation overwhelmed or having your stress action activated for too long. This is why it is still crucial to learn to unwind your body and mind occasionally and cut down on unnecessary stress whenever feasible.

Just How Can I Tell When I'm Too Stressed?

Stress and anxiety affects us all in different means, not all of which are adverse. When anxiety levels get too extreme, nevertheless, there are some tension symptoms that many individuals experience. Headaches, impatience, and 'fuzzy thinking' can all be signs that you're under too much tension.1 While not everybody that's under anxiety will experience these details signs, numerous will.

What Can I Do When I Feel Overwhelmed by Stress?

All of us feel overwhelmed every so often; that's typical. While it's essentially difficult to remove times when occasions conspire and also the body's stress response is triggered, there are ways that you can swiftly reverse your body's reaction to stress, buffering the damages to your wellness and keeping your thinking clear, so you can more effectively handle what's taking place in the minute.

Is There a Way to Be Less Affected by Stress?

In fact, by practicing a routine stress management method or more, you can eliminate some of the tension you really feel today and also make yourself a lot more resistant in the face of stress in the future. There are several various things you can try, varying from an early morning walk to an evening journaling method to simply making even more time for pals. The trick is to find something that fits with your way of life and also individuality, so it's easier to stick with.

ADJUSTING YOUR NIGHTLY ROUTINE TO IMPROVE SLEEP

It feels like rest should come normally. However when it doesn't, you could rapidly find on your own begging, "Help me sleep!" It can be a frustrating, unnerving experience to have actually sleep problems, defined by difficulty dropping or remaining asleep. You may exist awake for hrs in bed at night. When you stir up without feeling revitalized, this problem swiftly ends up being a drag out the rest of your life and health.

What are the reasons that you can not sleep? Are there reliable ways to help you to sleep far better tonight? What should you do if you have tried whatever, including natural home remedy, and it simply isn't functioning? Let's discover these problems and find the aid you need to sleep.

What Is Wrong With My Sleep?

We have an expectation of perfect sleep; that we will creep right into bed, sleep within minutes, rest without disruption and also stir up totally refreshed and also prepared to begin our day. Is this a sensible standard?

Kids are frequently hailed as a model of excellent sleep due to the fact that (generally) they are able to do just what we've explained. As we grow, our bodies change and our sleep appears to furthermore deviate from the ideals of youth.

Life, in a feeling, obtains made complex. There are new time stress, our rest is disrupted by others (consisting of bed partners and our very own children) and other illness (such as nocturia, heartburn and also pain) concession our sleep. As we get older, we might need less rest, with adults over age 65 requiring simply 7 to 8 hrs generally.

Therefore, we may not appreciate the rest we knew in our young people. Even the timing of our rest may shift. Those that remain in the twilight of their lives usually discover themselves waking early, incapable to remain asleep as they once did.

Some of our expectations concerning our rest might be somewhat misguided. As an example, the thought that we will drop asleep virtually immediately upon retiring to our beds might be incorrect. In some cases, this capability to drop asleep swiftly-- and enter fast eye activity (REM) sleep quickly-- can be seen in extreme daytime sleepiness that may occur in sleep deprival or narcolepsy.

Some rest scientists believe that it could be regular to be awake some throughout the night. When individuals rest in a group in close quarters, there is more time spent awake throughout the night. In background, fragmented sleep with durations of wakefulness in the center of the evening was common, mirrored in the twelve o'clock at night adventures seen in the plays of Shakespeare.

Several individuals get back to rest easily and also are untouched. The problem begins when our bad rest endangers our lives. If trouble falling or remaining asleep at night begins to have consequences, there is a motivation to look for the cause.

Common Causes of Difficulty Sleeping and also Insomnia

When we locate ourselves lying awake, watching the mins tick previous at a loss light of our alarm clocks, the desperation to sleep quickly escalates. There are many reasons this might occur, and also obtaining to the bottom of it may call for some representation on your situation.

The most typical factor why you can not sleep is additionally the most apparent: you are not tired. Your need to sleep will be significantly reduced if you are attempting to sleep at the wrong time. Problems with the timing of rest might happen in the circadian rhythm rest conditions, and in short-term conditions like jet lag.

You will additionally be subject to lengthy durations of wakefulness if you spend more time in bed than needed by your rest requires. Older grownups need much less sleep, so review how much rest you need and also just how much time you are investing in bed. An additional factor you might be diminishing your need to rest at night is that of naps you take throughout the day.

A very typical cause of trouble resting associates with stress and anxiety and also the invasion of boosting activities and substances. You may have trouble falling asleep the evening before a big examination or discussion. In periods of psychological stress, such as after the fatality of a loved one, you might likewise have trouble sleeping. This is called severe insomnia. It normally passes when these stressors deal with. Likewise, stimulants such as caffeine and also nicotine can disrupt your sleep.

You might be stunned to discover that exposure to light at night-- such as from a tv or computer screen-- may make it hard for some individuals to fall asleep. In addition, late-night cardio workout could rev you up and prompt insomnia.

For those who have chronic sleeplessness, the room area might come to be a trigger for sleep problems with conditioning. The sleep setting is suggested to be comfortable and facilitate rest. It must be amazing, silent, and free of distractions. Preferably, you would certainly not enable a tv or family pets in your room. Bed companions may be turbulent and also some individuals pick to preserve different rest areas consequently.

There are basic guidelines to boost rest. Numerous of these are implied to reinforce positive sleep routines. Uneven sleep timetables may set you up for sleep disturbance.

Lastly, there are clinical conditions that may be maintaining you from sleeping well in the evening. These may prevail troubles such as heartburn or discomfort, yet there are additionally numerous sleep disorders that might cause difficulty sleeping. A few of these consist of:

- Insomnia.

- Sleep apnea.

- Restless legs disorder.

- Circadian rhythm sleep conditions.

Whether or not you suffer from one of these conditions, you might be interested in discovering several of the treatment alternatives if you discover yourself struggling to rest during the night.

When You Can't Sleep, Home Remedies.

The very first task to rest better at night is to boost your rest health, which describes complying with the standards for far better rest. These actions might originally appear simple, yet because they include modifying your actions in connection with your rest, they can be difficult. You might be urged to look at other choices if you have understood these adjustments.

For those that have difficulty with insomnia, there are a handful of options to assist you rest. One treatment alternative is rest limitation.

There are various other non-medication alternatives that might be helpful. Some individuals discover advantage with making use of aromatherapy, although research studies may not support its use. Various relaxation strategies, including using biofeedback and also breathing techniques, may likewise develop a connection in between your body and mind. This can be integrated into your going to bed routines and make it easier to loosen up and shift right into sleep.

You may locate on your own turning to non-prescription drugs to assist your rest. One of the most typical is a normally taking place hormonal agent called melatonin. It can be extremely efficient if you have sleeplessness associated to an improperly timed circadian rhythm.

If you still battle to rest, you may be urged to consider various other alternatives, consisting of seeing a rest expert.

Major Professional Help for Difficulty Sleeping.

For those who still need assistance sleeping after tiring adjustments in your rest regular and at-home treatments, it may be needed to count on a rest professional. You may intend to start by talking about the issue with your key healthcare provider, however you may also choose a sleep medical professional.

There are diagnostic examinations that can be useful for examining your rest troubles, with unique examinations for sleep problems. It may be valuable to keep a sleep log or use an actigraph (like a health and fitness tracker) to track your sleep patterns. Additional testing with an over night sleep research called a polysomnogram can additionally be handy to recognize sleep apnea or uneasy legs syndrome as possible factors to sleep problems.

The various other benefit of talking with a medical care expert is that you can go over using sleeping tablets. There are 2 significant courses of prescription drugs that can help you rest: nonbenzodiazepines and benzodiazepines. The checklist of sleeping pills is long and consists of medicines like Ambien, Lunesta, Sonata, Trazodone, Belsomra, and others. These ought to not be used longer than a few weeks and if sleep problems persists, you might want to seek other therapy. Particularly, you can request a recommendation to a psycho therapist who may be able to educate you cognitive behavioral therapy for sleeplessness (CBTI) techniques.

While some degree of variation in mood is simply a part of life, they shouldn't interfere with the quality of your life. Be sure to allow your doctor understand if your state of mind swings don't boost or obtain worse.

How to use practices, such as mindfulness and meditation, to clear your mind and experience life as it is without judgment or negativity.

What Is Mindfulness?

Mindfulness is usually related to reflection technique yet it is more. It's a type of existing that can be exercised any time.

Mindfulness is the basic human capacity to be totally present, aware of where we are and what we're doing, and also not overly responsive or overloaded by what's taking place around us. While mindfulness is something all of us normally possess, it's quicker available to us when we exercise each day.

Whenever you bring awareness to what you're straight experiencing through your detects, or to your frame of mind using your feelings and thoughts, you're being conscious. and there's growing study revealing that when you train your mind to be mindful, you're in fact redesigning the physical framework of your mind.

When we purposefully pay attention in a kind and also non judgemental means, mindfulness is the awareness that emerges.

There Are Two Main Elements To Mindfulness:

Attention

Your mind is like an ape swinging from branch to branch. The ape mind typically assumes concerning the past. If your mind wanders to the past or the future you lose sight of the now and can not be present with what is happening right now

Mindfulness is focusing on what is happening in the present minute.

Attitude

Being kind and non judgemental goes to the core of Mindfulness method. This suggests that you approve what is and don't argue with the reality. This seems straightforward however when you start to practice Mindfulness you will recognize that you judge points and on your own regularly:

- We can not be late

- You are using the wrong shoes

- The home is such a mess

- What a grumpy waitress

- I simply don't like him

- Why can't I simply focus?

Mindfulness is about subjugating the internal critique, concerning erasing the should's and the should n'ts from your reasoning and coming to be much more accepting of exactly how things are in that minute. Mindfulness teaches us to be much more caring with ourselves, more caring and even more accepting of our experience. As we find out to exercise this, we become kinder and much more compassionate with ourselves and with others.

Mindfulness is exercising a kind and non-judgmental perspective in the direction of occasions, others and also yourself.

What Is Meditation?

It's an unique place where each and every minute is meaningful. When we meditate we venture into the operations of our minds: our experiences (air blowing on our skin or a harsh smell floating into the room), our feelings (love this, hate that, crave this, loathe that) and ideas (would not it be odd to see an elephant playing a trumpet). Mindfulness meditation asks us to put on hold judgment and also release our natural inquisitiveness about the operations of the mind, approaching our experience with warmth and generosity, to ourselves and others.

How do I exercise mindfulness and also meditation?

Mindfulness is available to us in every minute, whether through meditations and body scans, or mindful minute methods like taking time to stop and breathe when the phone rings as opposed to hurrying to answer it.

The objective of mindfulness is to wake up to the internal functions of our mental, emotional, and also physical procedures.

The Basics of Mindfulness Practice

Mindfulness assists us put some room in between ourselves and also our reactions, damaging down our conditioned actions. Below's how to tune right into mindfulness throughout the day:

Allot time

You do not require a meditation padding or bench, or any sort of special tools to access your mindfulness skills-- yet you do need to reserve time and space.

Observe the here and now moment as it is

The objective of mindfulness is not quieting the mind, or attempting to achieve a state of eternal calmness. The goal is straightforward: we're aiming to pay attention to today minute, without judgment. Easier stated than done, we know.

Let your judgments roll by

When we notice judgments arise throughout our technique, we can make a psychological note of them, and also let them pass.

Go back to observing the present minute as it is

Our minds commonly get lugged away in thought. That's why mindfulness is the method of returning, time and again, to the here and now minute.

Be kind to your wandering mind

Don't evaluate yourself for whatever ideas emerge, simply practice acknowledging when your mind has wandered off, and carefully bring it back.

That's the technique. It's frequently been said that it's really simple, yet it's not necessarily easy. The job is to simply keep doing it. Results will build up.

Exactly how to meditate

This meditation concentrates on the breath, not due to the fact that there is anything special concerning it, however due to the fact that the physical feeling of breathing is always there and also you can utilize it as a support to the here and now minute. Throughout the technique you may discover yourself captured up in ideas, feelings, seems-- any place your mind goes, simply come back again to the next breath. Even if you only return as soon as, that's okay.

A Simple Meditation Practice

Sit conveniently: Find a spot that gives you a steady, strong, comfortable seat.

Notification what your legs are doing: If on a pillow, cross your legs pleasantly in front of you. Rest the bottoms of your feet on the flooring if on a chair.

Align your upper body: but do not tense. Your back has natural curvature. Let it exist.

Notice what your arms are doing: Situate your upper arms alongside your upper body. Rest the hands of your hands on your legs wherever it feels most natural.

Soften your look: Drop your chin a little and also allow your look fall carefully downward. It's not required to shut your eyes. You can simply let what shows up before your eyes be there without focusing on it.

Feel your breath: Bring your attention to the physical feeling of breathing: the air moving via your nose or mouth, the dropping and rising of your stomach, or your breast.

Notice when your mind wanders from your breath: Inevitably, your focus will certainly leave the breath and also stray to various other locations. When you see your mind wandering carefully return your focus to the breath.

Be kind about your wandering mind: You may locate your mind straying constantly-- that's regular, as well. Rather than wrestling with your thoughts, practice observing them without responding. Just pay and also sit focus. As tough as it is to preserve, that's all there is. Come back to your breath over and over once again, without judgment or assumption.

When you're all set, carefully lift your gaze: (if your eyes are shut, open them). Take a moment and see any noises in the atmosphere. Notice how your body really feels today. Notice your emotions and ideas.

Mindful Practices for every single Day

As you hang around practicing mindfulness, you'll most likely find on your own really feeling kinder, calmer, and also even more person. These shifts in your experience are most likely to generate changes in other components of your life.

Mindfulness can assist you become extra playful, optimize your enjoyment of a lengthy discussion with a pal over a cup of tea, then relax for a relaxing night's sleep.

Practicing Mindfulness is a path to flexibility:

A major disparity in one's life is that the majority of us are creatures of habit and yet life on the other hand teems with shocks and also modifications. Occasionally occasions dismayed, hurt, infuriate and also temper us and we in turn respond in ways that no more offer our well-being.

Practicing mindfulness cultivates a greater awareness of the unity of body, heart and mind and brings one's attention to their subconscious thoughts, feelings, and behaviors that can weaken psychological, physical, and spiritual well-being. Scientific proof sustains just how living mindfully reduces anxiety, reduces blood pressure, boosts connections and enhances ones overall lifestyle.

Who's in control of your mind?

Learning to be alert in a non-judgmental method to what is taking place in the here-and-now, enables an individual to pick his/her response rather than being reactive to the experience life hands us. When you are being mindful you utilize your body and mind to do what no person else can do for you: take charge of your well-being, really feel much more in control and to live congruently with your life purpose.

Living mindfully does not imply that you need to meditate, come to be a hippy, take up yoga exercise and adopt Buddhist or Zen practices; it is about being able to be totally present to what you are experiencing in the moment and also booking judgment. Do you often feel worried, overwhelmed, pressured, angered or extended by what is happening? Visualize having the ability to go back, recognize your sensations, feelings and ideas, without judging them and to take a breath, approve, and ask "what is the best activity I can take for the most effective end result in this minute?"

Improve your self-awareness and act mindfully!

It might consist of, walking away, pausing from the task/activity, recognizing what you are experiencing in the minute, often calling what you are feeling utilizing assertive language (I feel ..., I think ..., I am ...) is very helpful; attempt utilizing assertive language to on your own out aloud to enhance your own self-awareness. When we live excessive in the past or spend excessive time staying in the future we frequently produce agony, disharmony, or sadness in our life. When we live mindfully we generally will establish a lot more realistic and possible objectives; goals that are supported by our internal & external sources.

Obviously it is difficult to live in the minute at all times. We need to prepare and also set objectives for the future and there are precise benefits in having the ability to reflect on the past; it assists to design etiquettes based on previous experiences and it likewise encourages us not repeat harmful habits and/or activities. Anxiety is healthy and typical and also proven to be a motivational motorist for many people, yet excessive anxiousness is detrimental to your physical and also mental health and the amount varies for each and every person.

Although we require to be able to reflect on the past and also prepare for the future imagine harnessing the skills to be fully present to what you are doing currently, completely present and also mindful to the experience, not limited by your past and not fearful of what might or might not eventuate in the future.

Mindfulness medication

In a common mindfulness meditation session, an individual sits on the flooring, eyes shut, back straight and legs went across, his body placed to facilitate his internal experiences. For 10 to 15 mins, he observes his thoughts as if he were an outsider looking in. He pays certain focus to his breathing, and also when his mind wanders to various other ideas, he brings his interest back to his breath. As he techniques, his mind empties of thoughts, and he comes to be calmer and extra relaxed.

Meditation has long been made use of for spiritual development. Extra lately, in psychiatric therapy, experts and also scientists have demonstrated rate of interest in a type of Buddhist meditation made to promote mindfulness, a state of being taken part in the moment without judgment. Mindfulness meditation has revealed pledge in treating conditions ranging from discomfort to psoriasis. However when it comes to treating detected mental illness, the evidence that mindfulness aids is decidedly blended, with the greatest data directing towards its capacity to reduce depression and also prevent relapses. In this column, we will certainly talk about these searchings for and several of the debates relating to applications of mindfulness.

Visibility And Acceptance

Individuals have practiced reflection throughout history. It has developed right into several kinds and is located in essentially every significant faith. In 2004 psycho therapist Scott Bishop, then at the University of Toronto, and his affiliates defined mindfulness as maintaining focus on present experiences and also taking on a mindset towards them defined by interest, openness and approval. Psychotherapy scientists have established and reviewed variants of mindfulness for therapeutic objectives. For example, mindfulness-based tension reduction acts, as the name recommends, to minimize mental anxiety. Mindfulness-based cognitive therapy, on the other hand, integrates mindfulness with techniques made to alter the useless ideas that might contribute to problematic emotions and actions. Both are generally supplied through eight regular courses and also an all-day workshop. As a remedy for anxiety and stress and anxiety, mindfulness reflection may help people release negative thoughts rather than consuming over them. Educating individuals to experience today, as opposed to reviewing the past or contemplating the future, may aid keep the mind out of a nervous or depressive loop. Without a doubt, some support exists for the effectiveness of such training in alleviating signs of depression and possibly stress and anxiety. In a 2010 meta-analysis (quantitative testimonial), psychologist Stefan Hofmann of Boston University and his associates checked out studies that evaluated both types of mindfulness reflection as a remedy for anxiety disorders and anxiety. They discovered that the meditation sessions resulted in substantial renovations in both conditions instantly after treatment, and about three months later. Provided the relatively handful of properly designed research studies readily available during that time, nonetheless, the authors were suitably careful in their verdicts.

Both sorts of mindfulness-based therapies were effective for depression and anxiety conditions, though not much more so than cognitive therapy without mindfulness.

Mindfulness has actually made out less well as a treatment for anxiousness disorders in some research studies. In an additional meta-analysis released this year,

that mindfulness treatments worked for anxiety but not for stress and anxiety conditions. The outcomes for anxiety might differ throughout examinations for various factors, but one possibility points to distinctions in person populations. Some researches consist of people afflicted with anxiousness conditions who also have considerable health problems such as cancer cells, whereas others do not. How well mindfulness jobs might depend somewhat on the resource of a patient's stress and anxiety.

Avoiding Relapse

The clearest mental health and wellness benefit for mindfulness may be in reducing regression rates for a subset of individuals with anxiety. Preventing relapse is a critical difficulty for specialists because regression rates for clinical depression are exceptionally high. Up to 60 percent of those that have actually had one depressive episode will certainly have several added ones; for those who have actually currently fallen back when, 60 to 90 percent will have additional episodes; and for those that have actually experienced 3 or more depressive episodes, 95 percent will regression. Mindfulness seems to be especially potent as a preventive in individuals that have actually slipped back 3 or more times. In a pioneering research of mindfulness-based cognitive therapy for depression recurrence, released in 2000, psychologist John Teasdale, after that at the Medical Research Council (MRC) in Cambridge, England, and his colleagues contrasted individuals getting treatment customarily, such as check outs to family members physicians, psychiatrists and therapists, with those who likewise received mindfulness-based cognitive therapy. Topics were followed for more than a year. Amongst those who had experienced 3 or even more episodes of clinical depression, mindfulness therapy significantly decreased regression prices compared to the usual treatment. No difference in between the teams emerged, nevertheless, for people that had actually experienced two or less depressive episodes. These surprising outcomes have actually been reproduced in several researches.

Although nobody understands specifically why the benefits of mindfulness would certainly be better for the example of 3 or more, a 2004 replication by Teasdale and psychologist S. Helen Ma, after that likewise at the MRC, supplies some leads. The researchers located, as Teasdale had previously, that in people who had actually experienced 2 or less depressive episodes, adverse life occasions, such as a death in the household or a connection break up, were a typical trigger for regression yet that such exterior occurrences were much less commonly connected with regression in those that came to be clinically depressed more than two times. The researchers guessed that by the time an individual has actually had 3 or even more depressive episodes, a significant adverse occasion is not needed for regression. Instead a strong association has actually been developed psychological in between even more average adverse state of minds and also depressive ideas. When a person who has actually recuperated from clinical depression experiences a light unfavorable mood, that state of mind may activate ideas such as "Here it returns," causing a full-blown depressive episode. In those cases, mindfulness could aid damage the cycle by allowing people to be much less influenced by fleeting unhappy thoughts to make sure that they do not cause emotional turmoil.

Through such devices, mindfulness-based cognitive therapy and mindfulness-based stress and anxiety reduction hold pledge as remedies for clinical depression and possibly stress and anxiety. What is more, mindfulness-based cognitive treatment offers clear benefits for stopping regression in clients that have actually had much more than 2 episodes of clinical depression.

Mindfulness and Mental Health

How You Can Use It to Lose Weight

You can additionally use this practice to assist you achieve and maintain a healthy and balanced weight.

With food, you have numerous chances to be conscious:

Do a gut check to see if you're really starving before you consume.

Focus on each bite, enjoying its taste and structure.

If what you're saying to on your own is valuable, Notice.

Do another intestine check to see how full you are. That way you can stop consuming when you feel full instead of mindlessly cleansing your plate.

Workout Your Mind

Intend to work out even more? Mindfulness can assist you appreciate activities. That, in turn, will certainly make you more probable to stick to them.

How do you exercise mindfully?

Listen to how your body feels. Are your muscular tissues strained? Do you really feel restless?

Does the activity you're doing make your body really feel good while you're doing it?

If the exercise targets a specific body component, just how does that part really feel while you're doing it?

Notice your thoughts about just how you're relocating. Are the thoughts urging?

When you focus on your body, it can motivate you to relocate extra throughout the day. You may likewise be much more pleased of your body and be kinder to yourself.

Mindfulness And Psychiatric Medication

What's the partnership in between mindfulness technique and psychological medicine? Can one be an honest mindfulness professional and, for example, take an antidepressant medicine?

These inquiries emerge typically and are important. They have a tendency to spark a lot of solid views. The inquiry is particularly relevant offered the rise in psychological medicine usage. Antidepressant use has broadened substantially: in 2000, 6.5% of the population utilized antidepressants. In 2010, that number had enhanced to 10.4%. The problem is close to my heart, and I picture that I have some predisposition around these concerns. I've been relocated by lots of mindfulness students explaining psychiatric struggles. Before training mindfulness, I spent years doing psychiatric therapy and study examining the effectiveness of medications for psychological problems. I've likewise seen loved ones battle with psychiatric distress and wrestle with the decision to take or forego medication.

My individual view is that psychiatric medicine has actually been unfairly stigmatized. Far from conflicting with one's practice, medication can play a vital function in sustaining mindfulness technique. It's crucial to acknowledge that psychiatric medications are incomplete.

That said, I assume the reflection community has actually been unnecessarily cautious of psychological medication. It's essential to bear in mind that mindfulness and medicines share similar goals: the reduction of distress. Whatever real tools we contend our disposal to lower distress are valuable. For lots of people, the strength of psychological distress can make mindfulness method essentially difficult. Supporting on a medicine in fact opens up the opportunity of resolving right into mindfulness technique. For problems such an anxiety, integrating medication and psychotherapy is typically above either treatment alone. In a similar way, for some individuals experiencing psychological distress, mindfulness coupled with medicine might transcend to either treatment alone.

I've been deeply touched by the healing that I've seen in students over the months and years of their mindfulness technique. But I've likewise been touched when I see someone battling psychiatrically who starts a medicine, and acquires substantial benefit. I do not assume that the alleviation stemmed from practice is somehow much more valuable than the relief derived from medicine. Sometimes I've seen individuals function so hard at their mindfulness technique, often doing psychotherapy as well, yet their signs and symptoms persist. They usually criticize themselves and envision that if they merely functioned tougher and also practiced extra, they would not endure as much. That attitude can be simply another form of self-harshness.

How are we to comprehend the suspect concerning drug? We seem to overstate the function of the will in psychiatric battle. This leads us to presume that laborious recovery-- treatments where we 'job,' like mindfulness-- is exceptional to other strategies.

Psychiatric medication is designed to alleviate suffering. Psychiatric drug is not usually created to promote flourishing. Mindfulness can reduce distress, but it can additionally lead us states of thriving and also a feeling of the deep efficiency of the minute.

Mindfulness And Positive Psychology

Mindfulness in Positive Psychology brings together the latest reasoning in these two essential self-controls. Favorable psychology, the scientific research of health and wellbeing and toughness, is the fastest growing branch of psychology, supplying an ideal home for the research and also application of mindfulness. As we ponder mindfulness in the context of positive psychology, significant insights are being exposed in relation to our physical and also psychological health.

If you have actually dipped your toes into favorable psychology, you have actually most likely found one of the more popular and potentially life-altering topics within the field: mindfulness.

What is Mindfulness in Psychology?

" keeping a moment-by-moment awareness of our ideas, sensations, bodily sensations, and surrounding atmosphere, with a mild, nurturing lens."

To take that meaning a bit further, mindfulness calls for a nonjudgmental recognition and acceptance of our ideas and feelings; acknowledging our sensations yet evaluating them (e.g., supplying a valuation like "I should not be believing that" or "That's a negative thought to have") would not certify as practicing mindfulness.

Mindfulness-Based Meditation

You might also hear the term "mindfulness-based meditation" when diving into the globe of mindfulness and positive psychology.

If you're wondering what the distinction is in between mindfulness and mindfulness-based meditation, there truly isn't much of one!

" Mindfulness" is commonly made use of when describing a general effort to include even more mindfulness into one's life, whereas "mindfulness-based reflection" normally refers to the kind of method that is seen as the stereotypical meditation-- resting cross-legged with closed eyes while participated in a reflection practice for an amount of time.

Typically, mindfulness and also mindfulness meditation refer to the same idea: remaining open and aware of your own inner operations and enabling your thoughts and sensations to occur without judgment.

The only distinction in between the two is that mindfulness meditation has the undertone of being a much more time-constrained practice (e.g., you dedicate 10 mins daily to it as opposed to practicing it throughout the day).

A Look At The Psychology Of Mindfulness

A question that is often asked about mindfulness is whether it's a state or a trait. This inquiry likely doesn't suggest much for the ordinary specialist, but the answer is actually considerable for anybody that dabbles in mindfulness. If it's a characteristic or toughness, it's something that is much more fundamental, extra long-term, and less adjustable; if it's closer to a state than a quality, it's more short-term, fleeting, and much easier to affect.

The argument still surges, yet we do recognize that mindfulness is absolutely not entirely on the trait side; studies have actually revealed that we can boost our mindfulness through concerted effort and training.

Nonetheless, we also understand that mindfulness is correlated with our strengths, so we possibly can not claim that it's totally on the state side either.

A Brief History Of Mindfulness In Psychology

Although mindfulness has been a staple of the positive psychology world for several years-- and a preferred subject in the wider field prior to that-- it in fact predates the modern area of psychology. It was initially a Buddhist practice called sati, which can be specified as,

" the moment-to-moment lucid awareness of whatever develops in the mind"

Dr. Jon Kabat-Zinn is thought about the "founding father" of the U.S.-based mindfulness fad. He was presented to mindfulness with his expedition of Buddhist viewpoint in his college days, which he then integrated right into his technique as a professor of medicine at the University of Massachusetts Medical

School. He founded the Stress Reduction Clinic at the medical institution in 1979, where he established the program that is recognized today as Mindfulness-Based Stress Reduction.

Since then, mindfulness has actually expanded in appeal and is significantly the subject of researches on ways to decrease anxiety, increase positivity, and also raise quality of life.

A Look At The Techniques Used

Right here are a couple of tips and also techniques to make sure you're obtaining one of the most of your mindfulness technique:

Pay very close attention to your breathing, especially when you're feeling extreme emotions.

Notification-- truly notice-- what you're sensing in a given minute, the sights, sounds, and scents that generally slide by without reaching your mindful recognition.

Acknowledge that your emotions and also thoughts are short lived and do not specify you, an understanding that can free you from unfavorable idea patterns.

Tune into your body's physical sensations, from the water hitting your skin in the shower to the means your body rests in your office chair.

Find "micro-moments" of mindfulness throughout the day to reset your focus and also feeling of objective (Greater Good Science Center).

Mindfulness And Clinical Psychology

Mindfulness is an outstanding method to practice self-care, that makes it an excellent tool that aiding specialists can show their clients to encourage recovery, growth, and healthy and balanced habits beyond the one-hour workplace brows through.

Mindfulness And Positive Psychology: What Are The Links?

Mindfulness has actually been a staple of positive psychology, copulating back to the structure of the area. It is not so much connected to positive psychology as it is interwoven right into its very material.

The close connections between mindfulness and favorable psychology make good sense when you take into consideration the results of mindfulness: increased positivity, a greater sense of comprehensibility, far better quality of life, more compassion, more rewarding relationships, and greater hope.

6 Examples Of How Mindfulness Is Used In Positive Psychology

Mindfulness is a multi-tool in positive psychology-- a practical method that has numerous uses and also is effective in a wide variety of contexts.

Here are just a few ways that mindfulness can be applied in positive psychology:

As a self-care tool for anybody that is interested-- mindfulness can be practiced by any individual, anywhere, anytime!

As a tension decrease method for students, people in high-stress tasks, and also anyone handling anxiety.

As a means to boost staff member health.

As a therapeutic device for individuals having problem with depression or various other mood problems.

As a coping technique and also leisure strategy.

Together with yoga as a healthy and balanced behavior for mind and body.

Great Benefits Of Mindfulness In Positive Psychology

There are many favorable end results that arise from developing and exercising mindfulness. Below are 7 of the most substantial and favorable advantages of mindfulness.

Bearing in mind your ideas and also feelings advertises health

The concept of self-regulation is rather paradoxical because guideline-- in the strictest feeling of the word-- is not actually considered being conscious; rather, mindfulness is a state that is identified by self-contemplation, self-acceptance, reflection, and openness.

The study is clear on one of the primary outcomes of practicing mindfulness: there has been strong proof appearing lately that demonstrates that mindfulness is significantly associated with positive affect, life satisfaction, and general well-being.

Mindfulness itself, however, is not a new idea; it has existed in Buddhism for over 2 thousand years. Contemporary research has actually made a number of fascinating searchings for suggesting this 'improved self-awareness' reduces anxiety and stress and anxiety and, consequently, reduces the risk of creating psychopathology, cancer cells, and also disease. It is useful to exercise mindfulness in positive psychology as a device for basic physical and psychological wellness.

Being conscious can improve your working memory

Functioning memory is the memory system that briefly stores information in our minds for more recall and also future processing. Several studies have been embarked on that recommend a strong correlation in between attention and functioning memory. Van Vugt & Jha (2011) embarked on study that involved taking a group of participants to an extensive month-long mindfulness hideaway. These individuals were compared with a control group that obtained no mindfulness training (MT). All individuals from both teams initially undertook a memory recognition job prior to any type of MT had been supplying. The second round of a memory acknowledgment task was after that taken on by all individuals after the month's training.

Results were positive-- while precision degrees were similar across both teams, reaction times were much faster for the group that had actually gotten mindfulness training. These results suggested that MT causes attentional improvements, especially in regard to quality of information and also decisional procedures, which are straight linked to working memory.

Mindfulness functions as a buffer versus the depressive symptoms related to discrimination

A self-report study carried out at the University of North Carolina measured the degree of discrimination experienced by individuals in addition to the existence and also-- if present-- seriousness of their depressive. Individuals also finished a set of questions that determined their level of mindfulness as a quality or toughness, which is characterized by a tendency towards mindful recognition of the present.

The outcomes showed that, as anticipated, the more discrimination individuals experienced, the much more depressive signs and symptoms they had. It was likewise found that the more conscious individuals were, the less clinically depressed they were.

and most importantly, the findings suggested that mindfulness could be a safety aspect that mitigates the effects of discrimination on the growth of depressive signs and symptoms. Simply put, although discrimination was connected with depressive signs, the organization became much weaker as mindfulness raised. According to research studies such as this one, it appears that exercising mindfulness may be an effective method of stopping the start of anxiety.

Mindfulness can help you make better use of your strengths

"Mindfulness can help an individual reveal their personality strengths in a balanced manner in which is sensitive to the context and scenario they are in."

Not surprisingly, mindfulness is associated to character staminas. In Buddhism, mindfulness reflection is not only an efficient technique of soothing suffering, it is also a means to grow favorable characteristics and also toughness such as wisdom, concern, and well-being.

Also the definition of mindfulness, defined byThichNhat Hanh, includes some measurements of toughness; his viewpoint on mindfulness states that mindfulness is an approach:

" to keep one's focus alive in the here and now reality. and this 'aliveness' captures both the self-regulation of focus and the approach of interest."

Experiencing mindfulness begins with making a commitment to preserve curiosity concerning the mind roaming and looking at differences in other things. Other study found that curiosity is one of the strengths that is associated to living a satisfied, purposeful, and appealing life.

According to a research study, transcendence strengths can come to be much more meaningful in mindfulness technique as they attach mindfulness with spiritual significance.

Furthermore, throughout the method of mindfulness, people may face both outside and also inner obstacles consisting of boredom, a wandering mind, physical discomfort, and problem in staying devoted to the method, and it requires a not-insignificant stamina of courage and also determination to conquer these obstacles and maintain going.

" Mindfulness opens up a door of understanding to that we are and personality strengths are what lags the door considering that personality toughness are that we go to core"

Mindfulness can also assist you make better use of your toughness; think about it-- how effectively can you seek your goals if you do not really take notice of your very own inner workings? Pursuing-- and also achieving-- one's objectives needs focus to be paid to inner states, feelings, ideas, and behaviors.

Therefore, to be able to see your toughness, you need to have access to your internal frame of mind. To access your strengths and your real self, mindfulness is the course.

Mindfulness can aid us move past these two obstacles. It can additionally decrease the bias we have in the direction of ourselves because exercising mindfulness can lower the defensiveness of your ego as you begin to have more reality-based thoughts. It turns out that the exact same is real for mindfulness!

Mindful awareness is a type of experience that changes not only framework, however also the function of our brain throughout our lives. Mindfulness can be taken a psychological muscular tissue. Every single time we raise weight, we strengthen the muscular tissue we are working on. Similarly, every single time we focus on today minute without judgment or efforts to manage, self-regulation and also compassion-related mind areas grow.

Mindfulness Practice Can Raise Your Happiness Set-Point

Our mind is separated right into 2 hemispheres: the appropriate hemisphere and also the left hemisphere. We understand that the appropriate prefrontal cortex (the front-most part of the mind that regulates higher functions) is very active when we remain in a depressed, nervous mood.

On the other hand, our brain has high activity in the left prefrontal cortex when we are happy and also energised. This proportion of left-to-right task shows our joy set-point throughout day-to-day activities. So, what happens to this proportion when we exercise mindfulness meditation?

The study of Richard Davidson and also Jon Kabat-Zinn shows that a straightforward 8-week training course of 1-hour daily mindfulness technique resulted in substantial boosts in left-sided activation in the mind-- a rise that is maintained also after 4 months of the training program. To summarize, this searching for shows that short-term mindfulness method increases our joy level substantially, right to the physical level.

Mindfulness Can Make You More Resilient

In the most fundamental terms, durability describes a person's capacity to recoup from problems and adapt well to change. The little corner of our mind that pertains to resilience is an area called the former cingulate cortex (ACC), which lies deep in the center of the mind. The ACC plays a crucial function in self-regulation and learning from the previous experience to promote ideal decision-making.

The research study searchings for of Tang and his coworkers reveal that mindfulness training groups that finished 3-hour mindfulness practice have greater activity in ACC and additionally reveal higher efficiency on the tests of self-regulation and also resisting distractors, compared to the control group.

This means that with simply a little commitment to practicing mindfulness, we can transform the method our brain responds to obstacles and enhance our capability to make wise choices.

It Shrinks The Stress Region In Your Brain

Have you ever before experienced a rough patch in which you hurry through your everyday life with perspiring hands and anxiousness, maybe even struggling to sleep during the night? Whenever we get stressed out, a little part of our brain called the amygdala takes control.

The amygdala is an essential stress-responding region in our mind and plays an essential role in assisting us cope with distressed situations. It's a well-known truth that high amygdala task is associated with clinical depression and anxiety conditions.

Fortunately is that mindfulness practice can really shrink the dimension of the amygdala and raise our stress and anxiety reactivity limit. Current research done by Taren and coworkers revealed a link between long-term mindfulness technique and an amygdala that is reduced. By practicing mindfulness, we can alter just how we react to demanding scenarios and also improve our physical and mental well-being.

Study On Mindfulness In Psychology: When Is Mindfulness A Bad Idea?

It might not be reasonable to claim that mindfulness is ever before a bad suggestion, but the advantages may have been overstated and the negative aspects-- as few as there are-- shook off.

These downsides and disadvantages consist of:

A minor decline in the capacity to recognize what is real and also what is not, leading to the possibility of false memories.

The possibility for discarding thoughts that are handy, positive, or crucial in a few other method.

The capacity for an evasion of challenging troubles and crucial thinking, relying on mindfulness meditation as opposed to exercising a solution.

Remarkably, there are numerous negative adverse effects (and some unfavorable straight results) that have actually been reported. They are unusual, however still real possibilities for specialists of mindfulness; these include depersonalization, psychosis, deceptions, hallucinations, disorganized speech, anxiousness, enhanced threat of seizures, anorexia nervosa, and also insomnia.

These are actual prospective results of mindfulness, the risk to the average individual is marginal. You need to have nothing to worry around if you maintain your mindfulness technique in check and make sure not to use it as an escape.

Benefits Of Mindfulness

You prepare your day while listening to the radio and also travelling to work, and then prepare your weekend. Did you see whether you really felt well-rested this early morning or that forsythia is in blossom along your path to work?

Mindfulness is the practice of purposely concentrating your focus on the here and now moment-- and also accepting it without judgment. Mindfulness is currently being analyzed clinically and has actually been discovered to be a crucial element in stress reduction and also overall joy.

If asked to describe the worth of mindfulness, you may wish to consider the adhering to concern, can you sit for one min and also completely silent your mind? Can you do this without feeling like you're appearing of your skin?

Mindfulness specialist Jon Kabat-Zinn has actually explained mindfulness as taking notice of the present minute with objective, while letting go of judgment, as if our life depends on it. The here and now is the only actual moment we have. And also, in fact, our life might actually depend on it. Among its many advantages, mindfulness reflection has in fact been confirmed to enhance telomerase, the 'caps' at the end of our genetics, which, in turn, can lower cell damages and lengthen our lives. Furthermore, study shows that mindfulness strengthens our body immune system, making us far better able to combat off diseases, from the flu to cancer cells. Mindfulness aids boost our concentration and minimize ruminative reasoning that contributes to the high degrees of anxiety that is so prevalent in our culture. Tension and ruminative reasoning are not only psychological health hazards, yet they are, quite often, the very symptoms that lead people to seek the assistance of a therapist. Why is mindfulness so useful to mental health and wellness experts?

Mindfulness is an incredible tool to help people understand, endure, and deal with their feelings in healthy ways. It helps us to modify our regular feedbacks by taking time out and choosing just how we act. In doing so, we discover exactly how our minds work, and also we are much better able to classify the sensations and thoughts we are having, rather of allowing them to subdue us and dictate our habits.

Because mindfulness presents a reliable method to get to know oneself, to minimize tension, and to stay in the here and now moment, cultivating mindfulness is a powerful method in treatment. For something, research study has actually revealed that therapists who practice mindfulness themselves have better end results with their individuals, even when they don't make use of mindfulness strategies in their therapy. Including mindfulness right into treatment has actually been reliable in dealing with numerous usual psychological health and wellness battles. Marsha Linehan was just one of the very first to incorporate mindfulness practices right into Dialectical Behavioral Therapy (DBT) with positive results. As it's been used more and more, mindfulness has further confirmed to help deal with individuals experiencing personality conditions and bi-polar condition. Mark Williams has actually created extensively on just how mindfulness can reduce the likelihood of recurring anxiety. Having actually shown such positive results, mindfulness has been integrated into clinical practice, with several therapists including strategies and also meditation right into their approaches.

When you educate a person mindfulness techniques, you assist them train their mind to observe their own thoughts, feelings, and feelings with an objective view. This need to be done with compassion, as people often tend to lose perseverance with themselves, especially in the early phases of exercising mindfulness or trying out reflection. By learning mindfulness, they are far better able to take time out and respond in an extra constructive method to dispute.

Mindfulness supplies a great device for establishing even more self-acceptance, which helps us build our empathy for others. It can bring us closer to the individuals we care around and also help us to disrupt self-sabotaging patterns we've embraced throughout our lives.

Instructing ourselves to relax and to be much more receptive than reactive is a method made possible via mindfulness techniques. Whether discovering to meditate or just to listen with ourselves at different times throughout our day, we are enhancing our capacity to feel more integrated and to show honesty. We improve our capacity to concentrate our attention.

Here is a checklist of the possible advantages of mindfulness:

A higher connection with the body, thus being able to act much better in it's rate of interests.

Boosted individual connections, as mindfulness helps put an examine automated reactions; it additionally allows us to pay attention better

A greater acceptance of frustrating ideas and feelings. Mindfulness likewise allows us to let go of these before they can develop and have an adverse impact on us.

There is growing clinical proof that regular reflection makes positive improvements to the means the mind functions and additionally other elements of the body.

Improvements to memory, focus and cognitive capability.

A remarkable decrease in degrees of anxiety and also anxiety.

A boosted capability to fall to rest at night.

A boosted partnership with pain brought about by learning exactly how to accept the discomfort and come to be extra tranquil with it as opposed to being locked in constant battle.

A general sensation of health and wellbeing.

An increase in productivity produced by being able to take care of distractions more effectively.

Increased imagination brought about by having the ability to let go of doubts that or else may be a limitation to imagination.

Mindfulness is a way of training yourself to focus in a particular method which can help you in your everyday life, job, partnerships and also total wellbeing.

Wellbeing And Stress Relief

Mindfulness entails focusing on the here and now moment without reasoning, allowing you to relax your mind and body. Being mindful may allow you to concentrate on and also appreciate what you have rather than taking things for given. The understanding and sensation of gratitude may aid you really feel renewed.

Without being mindful, you might merely respond to adverse ideas and also sensations. Practicing mindfulness might help you to become a lot more knowledgeable about your thoughts and sensations, and manage them in a favorable method. Taking control of your feelings and also ideas can help in reducing stress and anxiety and stress and anxiety.

Relationships

Being mindful may assist enhance partnerships. In an active life, you may obtain distracted during communications with close friends and household and also take them for provided. Yet if you analyze the relevance of these partnerships to you, you are most likely to offer your loved anothers attention.

Work

Being conscious at work means focusing on one task at once as opposed to multitasking. This makes it more likely you will have the ability to carry out a job well.

Wellness

Study recommends that mindfulness may help people cope with lasting health and wellness concerns such as pain, depression and cancer cells.

HOW TO GAIN A HEALTHY PERSPECTIVE ON HOW YOU SEE THE WORLD THROUGH INTERACTING WITH OTHERS, MAKING POSITIVE LIFESTYLE CHOICES, AND VIEWING YOURSELF WITH KINDNESS.

To be a true success we should have skillful individuals skills. The secret to successful relationships lies entirely in our ability to take the perspective of one more. Perspective taking is that all important skill of having the ability to check out points from a viewpoint besides our own. Point of view taking generates the mindfulness of compassion and also empathy to our relationships. When these 2 qualities exist in our interactions common regard, success and movement onward is assured

Problem belongs to human interaction. Political enemies, company competitors and arch opponents deal with and also disagree one another bitterly as a result of equally unique passions. A win-win situation is often not feasible. Normally, one will certainly try to find out even more about the challenger to predict or pre-empt his activity. The purpose is to strategise and also win in a zero-sum video game.

Even partners will deal with conflict, although the scenario is extremely various from that dealt with by adversaries. Companions who share numerous comparable interests, goals and also worths can sometimes locate themselves in disagreement.

Disagreements and also distinctions can occur between companions or individuals in close working, social or family members relationships. We can all remember experiences of conflict with an employer we respect, a coworker we like, a buddy we rely on or a family member we enjoy, or even with a political leader we sustain.

When partners remain in dispute, it is constructive to do less political strategising and also even more perspective-taking - by which I imply to think about how things appear to the other event.

PERSPECTIVE MATTERS

Depending on where we stand, the view of our living-room and also the important things in it can look extremely different. Similar to our understanding of the real world, perspective issues in our subjective experience of the social globe.

When seen from various point of views, the very same facts can have different significances. The viewpoint everyone takes on affects what is thought about outer or central, evident or unknown, and also lacking or even existing.

We attempt to offer a different point of view that has a much more full view if a person has a passage vision. Often, 2 point of views might be entirely contrary - yet each is yet completely legitimate in various methods, just like the views from contrary sides of a room.

What is practical and extremely meaningful to him may look unreasonable to us if we do not comprehend an individual's viewpoint. But if we are undergoing the same circumstance, we might behave just like the person did, and also assume it is flawlessly regular or the appropriate thing to do.

So, fact is what things in fact are, but a person's reality is what the person thinks and also feels it is, given the scenarios. The individual's fact influences his activities.

Research studies in the behavioural sciences have revealed that we do not see points as they are. We see points as we are, and how we are impacted by the occasions or scenario. We make analyses according to our ideas and previous experiences concerning ourselves and others. We give significances to things in the context of the scenarios we live or find ourselves in.

When we have actually adopted a viewpoint, it is difficult to put on hold or transform it. It is even harder to take one more's viewpoint that is different from ours.

This is mostly due to the human propensity called confirmatory bias. We see what we anticipate to see. We choose and interpret info in such a way that will likely confirm our point of view.

The exact same choice, picture, event or declaration can mean something really various to various individuals or groups. And also everyone is usually convinced that she or he right. Several misconceptions could have been prevented if we had asked: "What else could it imply?"

If we can see things in a different way, from an additional individual's viewpoint, we can have less solid arguments and also even more positive feedbacks to contentious issues. At the minimum, we will be extra mindful in what we do or state in a difficult situation to avoid escalating the negatives.

Can some of the remarks and also placements on recent concerns in Singapore gain from even more perspective-taking?

Think about the policy on the tightening of foreigner inflow, the corrective sanctions meted out to the staff dealing with the liver disease C episode at the Singapore General Hospital, or the tasks noting the first wedding anniversary of founding head of state Lee Kuan Yew's death.

On issues such as these, can we put on hold or get outside our very own point of view and try to see points from one more's viewpoint?

If we can and also when we do so, we may locate our very own perspective not as legitimate as we believed. We are currently able to resolve the differences much better due to the fact that we comprehend the various other viewpoint.

MISINTERPRETING A PERSPECTIVE

There are 2 main risks to prevent when we attempt to take one more individual's perspective.

The very first is the overconfidence that we are succeeding in seeing points from one more individual's viewpoint, especially when we truthfully attempted.

When our partner was displeased with our gift and twice as upset that we did not try to recognize what he or she wants, remember the time. The fact is we did try to take our partner's perspective, yet wound up with an incorrect one.

When they presume what an individual is feeling or thinking by observing the person's facial expressions and behaviours, Research has actually discovered that individuals are extremely inaccurate.

Individuals are brash that they have actually handled to obtain the individual's point of view right, as revealed by their own evaluation of their accuracy.

The 2nd pitfall is uncritically dealing with another individual's point of view as valid and utilizing it to manage the dispute. When the perspective is based upon incorrect assumptions, the repercussion is commonly a misleading conclusion and missing out on the real problems.

For example, a point of view on an incident may think that a leader had accessibility to an important item of info when he made a decision.

If this assumption is factually incorrect but not remedied or examined, the disagreements could end up with judgments regarding stability when the real problem might be details circulation.

It is nondiscriminatory to claim we value different viewpoints. It takes individual conviction and also political nerve to state the advantages and disadvantages of each point of view, specifically the degree to which it is invalid or valid.

1. Think of others.

If we are not self-indulgent), Whenever we are in the existence of one more it is natural to believe concerning what they might be thinking (. We observe them intuitively and also observe nuances such as what they are doing, where they are looking, and also what their body movement is suggesting. This helps us establish if we feel comfortable around them which assists us make a decision if we want to connect with them and exactly how.

If we feel comfortable around an additional individual we begin to assume more logistically, like if currently is a good time to speak with them, or if they appear not available or hectic so we can make a decision one of the most effective means to continue. All of this refined information acts to motivate us to speak up in the conversation or to make a decision to keep back for a more convenient time.

2. Psychological policy and also empathy.

Perspective taking relies not just upon our capability to share feelings with others, yet additionally upon our capability to regulate our very own emotions. To be efficient with others we must understand what may cause us so we can rapidly refocus ourselves on what is happening with the various other. The point is not to ask ourselves what we would do in any type of provided situation; it's to recognize and also try what another would certainly do when it comes to compassion.

, if our compassionate accuracy and also psychological law abilities are solid we are extra successful in our interactions.. We have the depth and also recognition to predict the perspectives, assumptions, and also objectives of others that may be very various from our very own. This develops an interpersonal connectedness which is built to prosper and also be successful since individuals feel listened to, verified and also understood on the other side people.

3. Properly reading other people.

The feelings are our point of view taking guides. They aid us to check out people. We normally track the actions of others to determine and also attempt what they are assuming, really feeling doing or intending. Our brains assist us by supplying us a social radar system which assists us figure out individuals's objectives and also intentions, even when our focus is not specifically on them.

By doing this our level of sensitivities are our staminas. These level of sensitivities to other individuals sharp our digestive tract instincts to the purposes of others and to sense any kind of possible emotional changes in them or the peripheral work environment. Since it aids us to determine exactly how we can most effectively reveal up in the communication, it is essential to trust what we intuit about the intents others.

4. Translating words.

Many people talk indirectly, which requires us to presume the actual meaning of what they are attempting to state. We all recognize too well that what an individual says is not constantly what that person actually implies.

What we make a decision to claim or otherwise state calls for that we interpret as accurately as feasible what the various other individual is trying to state. , if we don't comprehend or we can not get a clear idea of where one more is coming from it is vital to develop dialogue to obtain clarification.. Many conflictual situations develop from a misinterpretation of what one more is attempting to connect. As soon as interaction is clear, depend on is obtained and success is inevitable.

5. Valuing differences.

Perspective taking calls for the maturation to gain the knowledge and be respectful of another individual's personal beliefs. When we are disrespectful to an additional person and their belief system it is the quickest course to creating separation and also department between individuals. It is the best method to upset a vendor, coworker or manager.

It is crucial to remain highly attuned to the fact that not all individuals share our personal views and beliefs of the world. This implies recognizing what not to say as much as ways knowing what to claim.

6. Be familiar with individuals.

What you understand about where people come from and also how they became individuals they are is essential in determining what to say and do. We connect extremely in a different way with colleagues that have had years of experience as compared to somebody new in the market. Our mind functions like a compass directing us to locate our way around and via details to keep interaction progressing efficiently.

When connecting which is why it is irritating when we give too little or also much info for various other people, every person's mind is wired to be reliable. Individuals typically make the blunder of anticipating us to know them well enough to stay clear of communication blunders. No matter exactly how well we understand anybody, we are human. It is with these mistakes that we discover to locate a balance in each private connection we have. Each blunder can only enhance the success and also stability of our relationships while likewise benefiting our mindfulness and personal development.

7. Examine everyone's individuality.

It is simple to take pleasure in associating with all sort of individuals, however, the method which we relate to somebody has a great deal to with just how we view them to be as people. When we are around a coworker that is even more intellectual or significant it calls for a different communication strategy from us after that when engaging with somebody who is even more laid back and also easy going.

Somewhat most of us come to be social chameleons, making minor shifts in our behavior to fit the individuals and also individualities we are about in an effort to ideal connect to them. This social adaptation does not make us phony as long as it makes us all-round. It allows us to use lots of parts of our individuality to produce positive and reliable relationships. This type of shifting is what makes us effective with other people and more successful and also entire as individuals.

The method of point of view taking brings empathy to the psychological climate of the workplace. It has the greatest capacity to positively impact our capacity to prosper via connecting well to others. And to guarantee a foreseeable emotional reaction from them when we think of empathy it naturally helps us to customize our actions according to exactly how we believe others believe. This does not mean we regularly look for to please others. Clearly, our actions at times will certainly create frustration or irritation; it simply means we look for to feel sorry for others as best as we can to guarantee we create the most reliable communication which will cause effective connections. Success in life and service simplify efficient interactions, humbleness, self-awareness and also the necessary skill of perspective-taking. These components are the tricks to success of any kind.

POSITIVE HABITS IN PERSPECTIVE-TAKING

Along with staying clear of overconfidence and uncritical acceptance, we can take on three favorable behaviors in perspective-taking.

First, be inclusive. Truthfully take into consideration other viewpoints that are extremely different from our very own.

When we contrast opposing viewpoints, we may uncover resemblances. We can see if their different strengths and weaknesses can compensate and enhance each various other when we find distinctions. Drawing on both perspectives, a brand-new and much better point of view might arise.

Actually, inclusivity might be most important when differences between perspectives are based upon strong worths and also concepts. We believe in honesty, justness, meritocracy, racial and religious harmony, responsibility and policy of regulation. When we intensely seek our very own point of view driven by among these concepts or worths, could it be that the individual we have a difference with is inspired by several of the other values and concepts that are additionally dear to us?

We need to pay attention to just how a worth or concept is used to the certain context, and think about just how various other values and concepts might be relevant.

We can additionally be conscious that when our point of view is controlled by a worth or concept, we may end up behaving or arguing in a way that is not as valued-based or principled as we need to be.

Second, be interactive. Researches have actually revealed true empathy does not happen by simply visualizing what the individual is going through, regardless of exactly how hard we attempt.

We need to interact with the person by listening and asking to learn the concerns and situations as perceived or experienced by the person. This demand for communication applies to shut family members and social partnerships, but likewise relationships in between fans and leaders.

When followers and leaders are taken part in naturalistic interactions - in contrast to contrived ones - they are more probable to tell each various other what they genuinely think, as opposed to what they assumed the various other wishes to hear. Consequently, one can much better appreciate an additional's problems and also circumstances.

Over time, high quality interactions construct mutual count on, reciprocity norms, social communication and even shared values between leaders and followers. All these will motivate them to see points from each various other's perspective, and assist in problem resolution and partnership.

The converse is likewise real. We will certainly not like what we see when count on is low and also we take each other's point of view. Research has shown that in such scenarios, seeing things from an additional's viewpoint will polarise opposing views better and result in even more problem.

Strike an intermediate note in between subjectivity and objectivity. To truly empathise with another person's viewpoint, one requires to be affective in embracing that perspective - and this involves feelings and also subjectivity. Yet compassion must be accompanied by some degree of detachment to keep neutrality in reviewing issues and perspectives.

Detachment implies the capability to step back to see the bigger photo, like when we zoom out in Google Earth to fly around with a digital helicopter view. We lose view of crucial details on the ground when we fly too high. High-flyers must be delicate to their fast ascent as they seek the helicopter view.

They must understand when and how ahead closer down-to-earth - to see what issues below them.

If we can be much more inclusive, intermediate and interactive when we handle differences, many distinctions might converge. They come to be pathways towards typical or corresponding goals.

If we find out to see points from an additional's perspective and also use it adequately, we are most likely to avoid misconceptions, make it possible for positive conversations and attain win-win remedies.

DEAL WITH GUILT

Feeling that uncomfortable slide of regret down your belly is difficult things, but it does not necessarily have to be a poor point. There are healthy methods to take care of guilt that turn it from a feeling that you wish to escape from, to an emotion that uses possibilities. If you treat it with function, you can use it to change your poor behaviors, strengthen your character, find out lessons, and also develop your relationships. That could appear difficult when you think about the negative, hand-wringing feels you obtain when regret sets in, yet it's everything about exactly how you treat it as soon as you have it.

We usually experience regret after we've done glitch, and as a result of it imitates a red flag and doesn't let you escape your crap. It provides you a chance to learn from your mistakes and also to quickly right your incorrect, prior to points snowball out of hand. That or it supplies you a possibility to recognize you're acting too hard on yourself and to reduce up.

Are You Feeling Guilty?

Are you feeling guilty concerning something? Because you stopped working to live up to your personal expectations, maybe you're feeling guilty. Maybe it's since you failed to live up to other people's expectations of you. Maybe you did something painful to somebody else, or possibly you shamed a person or wronged others in some way. Or maybe it's all about you. You are feeling guilty since you didn't maintain an assurance you made to yourself.

Really feeling guilty typically stems from an underlying sense of obligation you have to other individuals. It could likewise stem from a set of unsettled issues, feelings and/or individual feelings of unworthiness. The sensations of guilt can occur from your refusal to accept your blunders.

No matter what the reason is for your guilt, it's crucial to keep in mind that you're really feeling guilty for a factor, and also this shame is informing you that you are heading in the incorrect instructions. See sense of guilt as an opportunity for you to re-examine or correct your habits, or also an opportunity to fix a busted relationship.

If you fall short to make the needed changes to your behavior, and maybe select instead to neglect your sense of guilt, then regret can conveniently turn into regret or pity. Shame might additionally lead to a state of emotional paralysis or confusion.

No matter how you consider it, sense of guilt is never ever an enjoyable emotion and commonly has some dire effects. It is an emotion you can work with effectively and also even gradually eradicate from your life over time.

Exactly how sense of guilt can influence your wellness

According to Dr. Mehmet OZ, who is a cardiothoracic surgeon at the New York Presbyterian-Columbia Medical Center, "Guilt can shorten your life. Sense of guilt additionally has actually been shown to raise cortisol degrees. Cortisol is an anxiety hormone that your body makes as part of its "battle or trip" response.

Researches reveal that negative feelings and also thoughts can boost the anxiety hormones, adrenaline and cortisol. These hormonal agents assist trigger your body to react when you run into a hazard or a difficult occasion. The problem is when high levels of these hormonal agents last as well long, you begin to become short-tempered and uneasy. You may also begin to experience high blood pressure, rapid heart rate, tension ulcer in your tummy and also inflammation around your body.

Other researches reveal that sensation guilty can impact your mental wellness and also wellness. How sense of guilt influences your mind relates to your thoughts.

Research study shows that feeling guilty rises negative attitude. This worsens if a person is currently struggling with clinical depression. When a person is in a depressive state and additionally battling with sensations of sense of guilt this leads to adverse cognition. This is when a specific really feels and informs themselves that they are worthless, they are not good enough or they are not loved.

Usually, the individual begins to have a negative viewpoint regarding themselves. They begin to have low self-worth problems. As a result, they become more clinically depressed and also as researches indicate this can result in self-harm.

Tips to stop feeling guilty

1. Don't punish yourself.

Even if whatever you did was truly bad, it isn't handy to penalize on your own. Everyone does something that they wind up regretting at some point, and the best thing to do is to gain from your errors and not repeat them.

While regret may create you to really feel undeserving of happiness, do not undermine your very own wellness as a charge. It will not make up for your mistake, and it will create a much more miserable scenario.

2. Forgive yourself.

In addition to asking other individuals for forgiveness, you need to ask on your own for forgiveness.

Being able to accomplish self-forgiveness after feelings of sense of guilt is vital to one's self-esteem, which is an important element of delighting in life and connections.

It is necessary to understand that you can forgive yourself while still understanding you were at mistake, similar to you would certainly forgive another person even if you understood they did something wrong.

You can really feel regretful of your actions, yet be compassionate with yourself and accept that it is alright to make mistakes sometimes. Possibly you did your ideal under the provided circumstances at the time. Don't be so hard on yourself that you deny on your own forgiveness.

3. Approve you were wrong.

If you did something that was hurtful or incorrect, you will have to take responsibility for it, but accept that you can not alter the past.

It is important to go through the procedure of recognizing why you were wrong, however after that you need to let it go. The more you focus on the fact that you did something wrong, the much more it will certainly trouble you and interfere with your life.

Regret is typically a situational emotion, and also it is nothing to get mad over. Either time will pass, or you will certainly just recognize that you shouldn't really feel so negative and you wind up sensation much less guilty.

You will certainly feel far better and your guilt will certainly be soothed if you are able to recognize the concern and take action faster rather of later. Not doing any kind of offsetting actions (like saying sorry) will enable bad feelings to stay, and might lead to anxiety and depression.

Approve that you were incorrect, apologize, and go on.

4. Seek expert assistance.

If you seem like your regret is greater than you can deal with, it may be time to consult with an expert. This may hold true if it is not feasible to settle your guilty feelings with the individual who was hurt, such as when one person dies prior to an additional can apologize for previous actions.

In situations such as this, psychotherapy might be proper.

Experts can offer clients with workouts to practice that will certainly aid them process their feelings. A therapist might even work with a group or a household to work out concerns of regret that influence more than one person.

For some people, taking a medication might be helpful or even required to restore their happiness and also self-confidence after a situation that ended in significant guilt. This is something that can additionally be gone over with an expert specialist to see if this might be the best path for you.

5. Keep track of your shame.

You will experience incongruence and distress when there's a difference between who you are and who you want to be.

Keeping a day-to-day journal is one of the most effective habit you can begin to try to repair this. You will certainly enhance your self-awareness and be able to find out just how the regret is affecting you if you can create down how you really feel each day.

Journaling will certainly also enable you to blog about all of the components of the situation that have actually led to your sensations of sense of guilt. By going over what you did step-by-step and weighing it objectively, you can better recognize if you deserve the internal turmoil that you are experiencing.

Using your journaling time to live in the moment and also track exactly how your feelings change gradually will certainly permit you to notice the incongruences in your life and recuperate from your shame. You will be able to find out the tiny steps you need to make to develops changes in your life towards happiness.

6. You're not meant to be excellent.

Nobody is excellent. Even individuals who you believe live ideal lives make mistakes. Intending to be excellent in any type of component of your life will never ever go rather as intended.

The trick to realizing that excellence does not exist is to approve you are a part of mankind, which every person else around you is also simply attempting their finest to make their means via life.

7. Inspect your actions.

Numerous of us tend to lay it on thick when it comes to sensations of guilt.

Sure, in some cases this is well should have, however typically, we exaggerate our punishment to assist us seem like we have actually done our component. Due to the fact that this is not healthy and balanced, you need to step back and also reassess your behavior to establish if the quantity of shame you're permitting on your own to really feel is appropriate.

This is where identifying the sort of regret you are really feeling (whether it is disproportionate or proportionate) is very important.

Is your regret creating you to really feel depression, stress, or anxiousness? If so, just how are these added feelings showing up in your actions? You absolutely don't want to make points worse than they already are.

8. Concentrate on currently.

Stop considering what could have been and also focus on what is. Remember, no quantity of rumination can change the past, so you are only increasing your stress and anxiety by going over circumstances in your head repeatedly.

Instead, concentrate on the present moment and live mindfully. You have control over just how you are acting and also really feeling right now, and also there is no use in including more anguish to your life.

9. Be conscious.

There are two manner ins which being conscious can help you take care of feelings of regret.

Initially, when you are practicing mindfulness, you are residing in the moment. This implies you are not thinking of your remorses or anything that happened in the past. You are only concentrating on the things in front of you in this actual minute.

Second of all, if needed, you can spend some time as you are practicing mindfulness to ask on your own questions and also observe your actions to assist bring awareness to your very own feelings of guilt.

As an example, one concern may be, "What can I do each day to show myself that I am worthy of moring than happy, and to assist construct a new foundation of authentic self-confidence?" Getting understanding of your feelings is the first step to taking care of them in a effective and conscious method.

10. Allow it go.

Eventually, you have got to just ask forgiveness and also allow it go. While you may still be facing the repercussions of a bad choice, you can stop consuming over them.

Quit giving yourself a tough time, and don't go overboard to try to please the person you injure or betrayed. Their mercy remains in their very own hands

Identify the adverse effects of holding onto the past and also simply let it go.

Final Thoughts on Dealing with Guilt

Guilt is an extremely usual feeling that everyone experiences.

However it is necessary to determine the type of regret you are managing. Be aware that not all feelings of guilt are purposeful and rational.

Bear in mind to always be doubtful when you feel guilty-- is the feeling trying to show you something sensible regarding your actions, or is it a severe response to an useless scenario?

Your response here is your initial step to aiding you deal with future sensations of shame.

There are repercussions when we do not address our guilt, such as sensations of anxiety, anxiety, and even depression. See to it that you encounter your misdeed and make amends so you can lock up any type of loosened ends with the situation prior to proceeding.

The steps above are a fantastic begin to address your shame and also discover exactly how to handle the regret in your life in a healthy way.

HANDLE HOSTILITY AND CRITICISM

It's hard to really feel fuzzy and also warm inside when our most recent Instagram post gets a pitiful two sort, let alone when our employer offers us adverse feedback on a task. But to do well in life, both personally and expertly, it's essential to take criticism in stride. Having the ability to hear people's viewpoints can boost our relationships, scholastic performance, and job satisfactionImpact of feeling responsible for unfavorable occasions on doctors' professional and individual lives: the importance of being open to criticism from coworkers. Aasland, O, G., Forde, R. The Research Institute, The Norwegian Medical Association, Oslo, Norway. Quality and also Safety in Health Care, 2005 Feb; 14(1):13 -7." > Trusted Source. Learn just how to handle what others have to say without shedding a tear.

Helpful or upsetting?

Objection is a term for judgment or assessment, negative or good. and it can pop up all over: from university documents, to personal blog sites, to family members parties, and chats with buddies. (Your new haircut does not match your face form. Have a terrific day!) There are great deals of reasons that individuals provide objection, like feeling jealous or troubled in a romantic relationship (You always neglect to call!). At work, company leaders may also make use of criticism to assist workers boost their job-- and make them tremble before approaching the boss's workplace. But not all objection is bad information bears.

Constructive criticism-- providing thoughtful feedback-- can help us obtain useful insight into our actions and also increase trust in between individuals. Among college students, positive criticism on scholastic job (Here's how this paragraph could be far better) might enhance that GPA more than deconstructive objection (This paper is horrible). Unsurprisingly, deconstructive objection can hurt individuals's self-confidence, making them really feel guilty for not carrying out up to the same level.

Your Action Plan

Being sensitive to objection can be a sticky circumstance. Sometimes individuals may also stop working toward a goal out of anxiety of being critiqued. Don't offer in to those worries concerning prospective critiques. Right here are some helpful pointers to manage any type of objection that heads our means:

Listen up.

Figure out whether the objection is constructive or simply impolite. You might feel injured when your partner claims you're controlling, however having him explain this problem may aid you transform and eventually save the relationship. Lend all ears and also try to discover from it rather of getting defensive if objection can be practical.

Respond comfortably.

Be considerate no matter what, and say thanks to a person if the responses is usefulTrusted Source. A basic smile makes you the bigger person.

Don't take it directly.

Attempt to eliminate yourself from the circumstance and focus on what's being critiqued. That C+ midterm doesn't show your A+ character! Rather, it's a tip to examine a little more challenging next time, miss all that partying the night previously, or realize that calculus simply isn't your largest stamina.

Handle tension.

We can feel out of control and incapable to respond to criticism with a clear head when we're frequently on edge. So take a deeeep breath to keep those stress levels in check.

Keep keepin on'.

Remember that the objection stands for simply a single person's viewpoint. Know what your staminas are and do not let other people's point of views keep you from working hard towards a goal. If somebody states you're also brief to be a power forward, begin working with that jump shot!

BUILD SELF-ESTEEM

When you really feel great regarding on your own it's simple to worth on your own and concern the globe as a wonderful location.

It's as well straightforward to think of that by simply informing a person to be favorable they will certainly begin to really feel much better regarding themselves, and also it is much from valuable to agree with them that all is ruin and grief. All of us have selection yet somebody with reduced self-esteem might not have the ability to see anything aside from the darkness of no self-esteem. The technique is to allow somebody to take duty on their own.

You can just enhance your self-esteem if you're very first prepared to test the unfavorable sensations and judgments you have towards on your own. No issue just how persuaded you are of your present analysis of on your own, you have absolutely nothing to shed and also the globe to acquire by thinking about that you have a lot a lot more control over your self-esteem than you assume.

The essential point to bear in mind while you are doing this self-evaluation, which might prolong over at some time, is that in practically every circumstance or problem, you can make selections that will certainly enhance your reasoning and also boost your life. and when you do, when you really feel in synch with what makes you distinct, your self-esteem meter simply may sign up some of its all-time greatest scores.

There are points you can do, right here and currently, to transform just how you really feel regarding on your own. Raising your self-esteem will certainly call for a mix of transforming the method you believe and also transforming what you do.

Exactly how to develop self-esteem consist of:

Concern terms with uninvolved/negligent authority numbers.

If your guardians or moms and dads aren't able to correctly care for you or provide you sustain and focus-- be it from psychological health and wellness or material misuse concerns or some various other reason-- it is definitely, favorably, 100% not your mistake. If you're in the regrettable situation of not being cared for effectively by a moms and dad or guardian, it's essential for you to take into consideration that the method you're being dealt with is not of your doing and is, in truth, unjust.

Coming to terms with uninvolved authority numbers does not imply not caring and not injuring due to the fact that of them. Self-esteem comes from you-- not others, not also those that are meant to care for us most.

That does not suggest that helpful and also caring authority numbers aren't crucial. Individuals that offer and function for these solutions do so since they care concerning young individuals.

Image having favorable self-esteem

While Steven's self-esteem was knocked by one huge occasion in his life, many individuals experience years and also years of reduced self-esteem. It might be tough for them to also regard what maybe like to assume much better concerning themselves, and probably also terrifying to visualize something that is so unidentified.

Do not allow stress and anxiety take control of your life - you can reclaim control

To aid conquer this obstacle, attempt responding to the concern what would certainly it resemble to have favorable self-esteem? You can address by listing brief sentences; composing a tale or tune, or by illustrating.

Steven's actions to the above inquiry were: "Celebrating your accomplishments"; "Knowing on your own - the great and the negative, and being alright with it"; "Being satisfied with YOU" and

"Seeing that every person has defects, also individuals you assumed were best (there is no such point as best)".

You can begin functioning on developing it for on your own as soon as you have actually thought of the kind of sensations that can occur from having favorable self-esteem.

Pick positive peers.

It's simple to select close friends based on that's most preferred; while this group might enhance your social standing, it can likewise belt your self-esteem when your "pals" place you down or motivate you to do points you're not comfy with or proud of. Bordering on your own with encouraging buddies that care concerning you can assist you keep a healthy and balanced degree of self-esteem.

Obtain aid for injury.

Therapy for injury is extremely vital. If you're not comfy chatting with moms and dads or guardians regarding injury, take into consideration inquiring if you can see a specialist or therapist for factors you would certainly instead schedule for personal sessions. Take into consideration chatting with a college advice therapist or various other relied on grown-up regarding it if a person in your residence is harming you or has actually injured you.

Beginning considering your body in a different way.

When assumed around from this point of view, there is no perfect body kind. The means your body looks and also what others believe of it end up being much less essential than just how well it operates.

If you see it as an item for others, it is most likely that you aren't utilizing your body as the valuable tool it is. The company About-Face records that a research located women and girls that externalized their bodies to show poorer electric motor efficiency than women and girls that really did not externalize their bodies. Scientist asked women aged 10-17 to toss a softball as tough as they might versus a far-off wall surface; those that saw their bodies as items and also were really worried regarding their look did improperly contrasted to those that really did not externalize their bodies.

Professional dancer jumping

Young ladies aren't most likely to establish solid, healthy and balanced and qualified bodies when they're much more concentrated on just how they look than just how well their bodies work. Youthful guys, on the various other hand, might assume that muscle stamina or total mass is the most vital point concerning their bodies.

Both males and also females with body photo problems run the threat of counting on their bodies to prove to their worth, instead than utilizing them as tools with which to go after beneficial objectives in the globe. When you make healthy and balanced adjustments, however, you're promptly aiding your body job much better.

Obtain associated with something larger than on your own.

One of the finest methods to locate definition in your life is to obtain included in something larger than on your own, to have a result on the globe around you. Certain, you might have whole lots in usual with several individuals, however none of them has your precise viewpoint, experience, objectives, passions and also wishes.

The advantages of this action are best explained via the tale of my young pal, Stacy:

Stacy was distressed by this, so she and also a close friend chose to function to alter it. Stacy fulfilled with one of her neighborhood agents, that went on to discover numerous enrollers for what would certainly end up being House Bill 88, an item of regulations that Stacy and her good friend prepared.

I asked Stacy just recently exactly how having such an effect on her state legislations influenced her self-esteem. She claimed, "I made a distinction when I was simply 17, yet what many individuals do not recognize is that any person can do that.

Doing terrific points, subsequently, can bring about terrific sensations regarding on your own. Young person can use their power by focusing on what impassions them and also speaking with grown-up advisors or investigating individuals ready of power to get in touch with in order to articulate their ideas, point of views, issues and also suggestions.

Establish sensible objectives.

Reasonable objectives establish you up for a feeling of success, for something to be pleased of. Rather of anticipating on your own to obtain all A's following term, attempt establishing a much more possible objective, such as locating a tutor or coach to aid you with the topics you have a hard time with the majority of.

Whether it's trainee council, the college paper, the yearbook board, a sporting activity or cinema, you're component of a group. Do not attempt to be much better than others.

Established practical social objectives. Objective for growing a couple of significant partnerships instead than a wide variety of superficial ones.

Use positive affirmations correctly

Since when our self-esteem is reduced, such statements are merely also in contrast to our existing ideas. Paradoxically, favorable affirmations do function for one part of individuals-- those whose self-esteem is currently high. For affirmations to function when your self-esteem is delaying, fine-tune them to make them a lot more credible.

Determine your proficiencies and create them

Self-esteem is developed by showing actual capacity and success in locations of our lives that matter to us. If you satisfaction on your own on being an excellent chef, toss even more supper celebrations.

Discover to approve praises

One of the trickiest facets of enhancing self-esteem is that when we really feel poor regarding ourselves we often tend to be extra immune to praises-- also though that is when we most require them. In time, the impulse to refute or rebuff praises will certainly discolor-- which will certainly additionally be a wonderful sign your self-esteem is obtaining more powerful.

Get rid of self-criticism and also present self-compassion

When our self-esteem is reduced, we are most likely to harm it also better by being self-critical. Doing so will certainly prevent harmful your self-esteem even more with important ideas, and assist construct it up rather.

Verify your genuine well worth

The complying with workout has actually been shown to aid restore your self-esteem after it received a strike: Make a listing of high qualities you have that are purposeful in the details context. If you obtained denied by your day, checklist high qualities that make you a great partnership possibility (for instance, being mentally readily available or faithful); if you fell short to obtain a job promo, listing top qualities that make you a beneficial staff member (you have a solid job values or are accountable).

Forgive on your own.

When we've made numerous negative selections in the past, as defined in the last area, we can start to really feel that we're simply "that kind" of individual. It's vital to forgive on your own-- not to allow on your own "off the hook," yet to approve that some of the options you've made were not the finest and also fix to do far better in the future.

Obstacle unfavorable idea patterns.

Damaging the cycle of adverse idea patterns needs some perseverance, however the procedure is rather straightforward. Beginning by recognizing unfavorable ideas-- "I can not do that," "That individual possibly dislikes me," are some instances.

Recognize triggers-- To boost the degree of favorable reasoning in your daily life, you initially have to acknowledge what individuals, points, and areas advertise adverse reasoning. That begins with paying interest to what makes you really feel nervous or depressing.

Take notes-- There's a recurring discussion, or "self-talk," constantly occurring in your mind as you go around your day. This self-talk takes in the globe around you and makes examinations regarding on your own and others.

Next off, work with various means to translate scenarios. "That will certainly be hard, yet I can try it out," or, "I'm not exactly sure just how that individual really feels regarding me, yet I appreciate him/her and also wish to deal with being pals." By changing ungrounded adverse ideas with even more positive and also reasonable ones, you provide on your own an opportunity whereas prior to you would certainly have surrendered or otherwise attempted-- you make it feasible to confirm your old unfavorable ideas incorrect.

Obstacle your reasoning-- If you see on your own leaping to verdicts, or constantly minimizing the favorable regarding on your own, after that you need to step up and include some hopefulness to your self-talk. Finding out to concentrate on the favorable and to motivate on your own is a great deal like a reinforcing a muscle mass. You need to exercise your mind a little on a daily basis to establish an ability for hopefulness, to forgive on your own when you make errors, and also to find out to provide on your own credit history when you complete an objective.

One more means to neutralize adverse ideas concerning on your own is to make a listing of your toughness. Make a listing of your staminas (and also passions)-- this might appear hard, yet press on your own to recognize as several as you can-- at the very least 5.

Individuals with reduced self-esteem will certainly frequently have adverse self-talk. They might inform themselves points like "I'm dumb, so should not also attempt" or "I'll never ever obtain a partner in a million years". Occasionally the messages individuals inform themselves resemble messages they might have been informed by overly-critical moms and dads, or by harasses, and also have actually in some way sealed these messages as real in their minds.

Do not allow purposeless or unfavorable ideas rule your life

To test adverse reasoning, you require to initially be conscious of it. Ask on your own (and also possibly create down) what words you make use of when you speak regarding on your own to various other individuals.

Currently consider what proof there is to sustain the messages you have regarding on your own, and what proof there is that does not sustain them? What would certainly be an option, or even more practical message? Probably a much more well balanced message?

He informed himself he would certainly never ever have an additional connection as he was also awful, and that no one valued him as he was foolish. When he composed down his ideas on paper, it was a little bit of a shock for him to check out exactly how severe he was being with himself.

Functioning with the proof workout, Steven came up with a much more sensible message to offer himself: "I will certainly have one more connection, when the time is. I have numerous qualities that make me excellent guy product, and also the ones I'm looking for in somebody else are not all to do with looks.

When you're exercising them in day-to-day life, the workout above will certainly aid you come to be a lot more conscious of your rate of interests and also toughness. Possibly you'll discover that a few of your toughness aren't obtaining worked out or you're not creating your rate of interests; because situation, think of exactly how you can do a far better task of concentrating on and also using these, and also maintain your checklist up-to-date.

Adjust the important things you can, and approve the important things you can not.

All of us have points we do not such as concerning ourselves, points we want could be various. Occasionally it is feasible to do something regarding these facets of ourselves. If you feel you are constantly late to fulfill good friends, see if establishing your watch 10 mins very early aids you leave home a little bit previously.

Rather of wanting you can transform points concerning you that are not feasible to transform, assume regarding exactly how you can change the method you see those points. Can you believe of any type of function versions that may have comparable features?

Be proud.

We all have a right to really feel excellent regarding ourselves, in the very same method we observe and value excellent points regarding individuals we are close to. What are 2 points you can call that make you really feel great regarding on your own?

Can you consider a time you did something kind for somebody else, and also really felt great regarding it? Attempt creating a paragraph concerning the experience, draw or doodle regarding it, or create a tune regarding exactly how it really felt.

Detail 3 points you accomplished in the recently, or checked off a 'To-Do List'. They do not need to large points - removing some scrap e-mails, completing a college project and also experimenting with a brand-new dish in the house are instances of accomplishments, as are rising promptly or returning a collection publication.

Acknowledge Successes.

Typically individuals with reduced self-esteem will certainly disregard their successes as good luck or opportunity. Individuals with high self-esteem take the time to commemorate their success.

Provide your success.

Consider all things you've achieved, after that compose them down. Make a listing of whatever you've done that you really feel happy with, whatever you've succeeded. When you require a suggestion of your capacity to obtain points done and to do them well, Review your checklist.

Obtain clear on your worth's.

Establish what your worth's are and analyze your life to see where you're not staying in placement with what you think. Make any type of required modifications. The even more you understand what you represent, the a lot more positive you will certainly be.

Stop Listening to Your Inner Critic

The important inner guide is that interior viewer that hurtfully courts our activities and ideas. This unpleasant internal doubter constantly nags us with a battery of unfavorable ideas concerning ourselves and individuals around us. It annihilates our self-esteem on a constant basis with ideas like ...

• " You're dumb."

• " You're fat."

• " Nobody likes you."

• " You must be quiet. Each time you chat you simply humiliate on your own."

• " Whycan not you resemble other individuals?"

• " You're useless."

In order to get rid of reduced self-esteem, it is crucial that you test these unfavorable ideas and stand up to your internal doubter. You can select not to pay attention to your internal doubter's personality murders or poor recommendations.

One method to do this is to document all your internal movie critic's objections on one side of a piece of paper. Compose down an extra caring and practical evaluation of on your own on the various other side. If you compose a self-criticism like "You're dumb," you can after that create, "I might battle at times, however I am qualified and also clever in numerous means."

Testing your internal movie critic assists quit the pity spiral that feeds right into reduced self-esteem. You can start to resist this internal movie critic and see on your own for that you truly are when you identify the essential internal voice as resource of your unfavorable self-attacks.

Begin Practicing Self-Compassion

In numerous methods, the remedy for self-criticism is self-compassion. Research study has actually revealed that self-compassion is also much better for your psychological wellness than self-esteem.

Dr. Kristen Neff, that looks into self-compassion, discusses that self-compassion is not based upon self-evaluation or reasoning; instead, it is based upon a consistent perspective of compassion and also approval towards on your own. While this might seem easy, treating on your own with empathy and generosity might be testing at. You will certainly create even more self-compassion as you exercise over time.

Below are the 3 actions for exercising self-compassion:

1) Acknowledge and also observe your suffering.

2) Be kind and caring in action to suffering.

3) Remember that flaw belongs to the human experience and also something most of us share.

Quit Comparing Yourself to Other People

Looking to increase your self-esteem by gauging on your own versus others is a huge error. Social media just worsens this issue, as individuals publish their glossy accomplishments and picture-perfect minutes, which we contrast to our stained, flawed day-to-day lives.

In order to construct a healthy and balanced feeling of self-esteem, we require to quit contrasting ourselves to others. Rather than bothering with just how you come up to individuals around you, think of the sort of individual you intend to be. Establish objectives and also do something about it that follow your very own worths.

Various other individuals can not be the requirement when it comes to your self-esteem. Social media definitely does not aid, as scientists have actually located that individuals that examine social media really often are extra most likely to endure from reduced self-esteem. Advise on your own that individuals normally just share the finest components of their life online.

Be Inspired

Think about some favorable words you've spoken with a track or a flick, create them out and also placed them someplace you'll see daily, like on a Post-it on the restroom mirror in the house, or in a framework following on your night table.

Evoke somebody that has actually been a favorable impact on you (this can be somebody you recognize, or a person you recognize of, consisting of a personality in a publication!). Assess what top qualities they have that you appreciate, and what you can gain from them. Can you think about whenevers when you revealed comparable high qualities, or can you envision an event when you might such as to show comparable actions?

Exercise Self-Care

Consuming healthy and balanced and working out likewise can raise favorable reasoning and also assist you really feel extra urged concerning your future. If you invest time with individuals that care concerning you, you might locate that instantly it's much easier for you to care for on your own.

Master a brand-new ability.

You raise your feeling of expertise when you end up being competent in something that matches with your passions and also skills.

Do something imaginative.

Imaginative jobs are a terrific method to place the circulation back right into your life. When you include the difficulty of attempting something brand-new, it assists you also a lot more.

Stand at side of your convenience area.

Stretch on your own and relocate to the side of your convenience area. Obtain uneasy-- attempt something brand-new, satisfy various individuals or strategy a circumstance in an unusual method. Self-esteem starts beside your convenience area.

Aid a person.

Utilize your abilities, skills and capacities to aid others. Provide a person straight aid, share valuable sources or instruct somebody something they intend to find out. Deal something you succeed as a present to somebody.

Recover your past.

Unsettled problems and dramatization can maintain you entraped in reduced self-esteem. Look for the assistance of an experienced therapist to assist you recover the past so you can relocate onto the future in a fearless and positive means.

Stop worrying about what others think.

You never ever really feel complimentary to be totally on your own when you fret concerning what others will certainly assume of you. Make a company choice to quit stressing over what other individuals believe-- start choosing based upon what you desire, not what you assume others desire from you.

Review something inspiring.

A terrific method to get even more self-esteem is to review something that raises you up and makes you really feel favorable concerning on your own.

Redeem your stability.

Specify what honesty indicates for you, and make certain that you're residing in conformity with that said understanding. It will certainly drain you and also leave you really feeling negative regarding on your own if your life isn't lined up with your personality.

Allow unfavorable individuals go.

If there are individuals in your life that are adverse--
that have absolutely nothing favorable to state or that
place you down or benefit from you-- do the wise
point and also let them go. The only means to discover
your self-esteem is to border on your own with
encouraging favorable individuals that appreciate you
and also worth you.

Draw the line in the sand.

The finest means to discover your self-esteem is to
produce individual limits. Know what your limits are
and just how you want to react when individuals cross
them.

Meet Your Own Moral Code

Confidence and self-esteem are improved dignity. If
you live a life that remains in line with your very own
concepts, whatever they might be, you are more
probable to regard on your own, really feel even more
positive, and also do better in life. A research at the
University of Michigan located that pupils "that based
their self-esteem on interior resources-- such as being a
virtuous individual or sticking to ethical requirements-
- were discovered to obtain greater qualities and much

less most likely to utilize alcohol and medicines or to establish eating problems."

To really feel great concerning on your own, it is vital to have stability and make certain that your activities match your words. It is useful to assume concerning your core concepts and act in line with those ideas when you are attempting to enhance your self-esteem.

Respect your look.

You feel your ideal when you look your finest. Gown like a person that has self-esteem and also allow your confidence come through in just how you look.

Invite failing as part of development.

When you've fallen short, it's a common response to be hard on yourself. If you can shift your thinking to understand that failure is an opportunity to learn, that it plays a necessary role in learning and growth, it can help you keep perspective. Keep in mind also that failing implies you're making an initiative.

Constantly stay a pupil.

Think about on your own as a long-lasting student. Strategy every little thing that you finish with a trainee's mindset-- what Zen Buddhists call Shoshin or "novice's mind"-- open, excited, willing and unbiased to find out.

Face your worry.

Enable on your own to really feel terrified yet maintain going anyhow. Self-esteem is typically discovered in the dancing in between your inmost wishes and also your best concerns.

End up being an advisor.

Be there for somebody that requires your support, your management and also your assistance. Their regard and also gratefulness-- and also viewing them advance with your aid-- will certainly contribute to your self-esteem and also self-esteem.

Specify success.

Clarify what success indicates to you and also what it suggests in regards to your self-esteem. , if you really want to do something you will have to find the self-esteem within yourself to just do it.

Reside in the minute

When you are concentrated on the minute, you can select your activities knowingly and also sensibly, untouched by the harms of your past and also unconcerned by fears or really hopes regarding the future.

Create understanding

When we're mindful, we can identify just how we are reacting and responding to our very own anxieties, producing a minute in between our feelings and our activities. We can after that pick to react in a much healthier method.

Write in a journal

A number of our feelings and thoughts are secured our subconscious mind and writing can assist to bring them right into our recognition. Discussing the means we think and feel can assist to different unfavorable suggestions concerning ourselves from the reality of that we truly are.

Be non-judgemental

When we approach our lives non-judgmentally, we just approve ourselves, our experiences, our successes and failures and also other individuals equally as they are, neither bad nor good, without satisfaction or embarrassment.

Keep linked to on your own

Mindfulness can assist you to create a feeling of link to on your own and lower your people-pleasing methods by permitting you to quit the auto-pilot reasoning and practices that maintains you leaping to please others without thinking about your very own demands.

Technique conscious reflection

Reflection simply implies releasing the auto racing ideas in your mind and also approving that those beliefs, feelings and thoughts are short-term, instead of parts of on your own. Take a couple of minutes on a daily basis to just be still, concentrate on your breathing and also enjoy your concerns drift away like clouds.

Take part in your very own life

Mindfulness urges us to come to be assertive and active in developing our very own lives. Understanding of your ideas and selecting your reactions to them allows you to act and also take part in your very own life.

Establish a novice's mind

When you have a novice's mind, you consider points as if you are seeing them for the very first time, with visibility, enthusiasm and flexibility from assumption. You can see points in a brand-new light, as opposed to immediately reacting with the usual patterns of practices.

Release

Non-attachment, or releasing, is the objective of mindfulness. You can trust yourself and choose what's right for you when you let go of what you think you should do or who you should be.

Change the perfectionism.

Couple of idea practices can be so damaging in every day life as perfectionism.

Because you become so afraid of not living up to some standard, it can paralyze you from taking action. Therefore you postpone and you do not obtain the outcomes you desire. This will certainly make your self-esteem sink.

Or you act however are never ever or really seldom pleased with what you achieved and also your very own efficiency.

Therefore your viewpoint and sensations concerning on your own come to be increasingly more adverse and also your inspiration to act plummets.

How can you overcome perfectionism?

A couple of points that assist are:

Merely go for excellent sufficient rather. Just understand that there is something called excellent sufficient and when you are there after that you are ended up.

Keep in mind that buying into misconceptions of excellence will certainly injure you and individuals in your life. This easy tip that life is not such as in a tune, a publication or a motion picture can be excellent truth check whenever you are imagining of excellence. Due to the fact that truth can encounter your assumptions when they run out this globe and injury and even potentially result in completion of connections, tasks, jobs and so forth.

Invest even more time with helpful individuals (and much less time with damaging individuals).

Even if you concentrate on being kinder in the direction of other individuals (and on your own) and also on changing a perfectionism behavior it will certainly be tough to maintain your self-esteem up if one of the most essential impacts in your life drag it down on a once a week or day-to-day basis.

Make modifications in the input you obtain.

Pick to invest much less time with individuals that fidget nit-pickers, unsupportive or unkind of your objectives or desires.

and invest even more time with favorable, uplifting individuals that have extra human and also kinder requirements and also means of thinking of points.

and consider what you review, pay attention to and see also. Invest much less time on a net online forum, with checking out a publication or seeing a TV-show if you feel it makes you uncertain of on your own and also if it makes you really feel extra adversely in the direction of on your own.

Invest the time you made use of to invest on this info resource on for instance analysis publications, blog sites, sites and also paying attention to podcasts that aid you and that make you really feel excellent concerning on your own.

Keep in mind the whys of high self-esteem.

What is a straightforward method to remain constant with doing something? As discussed over: to bear in mind one of the most crucial reasons you are doing it.

Advise on your own of the whys at the begin of this write-up to aid on your own to remain determined to function on your self-esteem and also to make it a necessary concern.

Doing this straightforward point and also maintaining these effective factors in mind has actually done marvels for me. I wish it can do the exact same for you.

Keep in mind that finding out favorable reasoning and establishing healthy and balanced way of life approaches aren't going to be overnight wonders. Being kind to on your own and also enhancing your feeling of self-respect takes technique, perseverance, and also time.

LITTLE THINGS YOU DO CAN KEEP YOU IN A GOOD MOOD ALL THE TIME

Sometimes life passes us by so rapid that it really feels as though we are sitting in a train with our life moving by like the landscapes outside the home window. We can start to feel like we are in a rut, and our life is being established by others.

There are a number of things we can do to locate the silver lining in our days. We can make little changes and also method self-care with nurturing practices. By cultivating excellent behaviors, we reveal our love and also respect for ourselves throughout the day, and these little details can maintain us in an excellent state of mind regularly.

1. Have sufficient sleep

Rest deprivation creates us to be foggy-headed and also not able to make good choices in the short-term. And also in the long run it has a variety of bad effects on our health. Sleeping sufficient maintains us in a great mood and keeps our spirits high. As an incentive, you can ensure that you have a delightful going to bed regimen.

2. Exercise

Workout provides us a rush of endorphins, and also therefore, supercharges our great mood. We understand that exercising is a necessary aspect of self-care. So pull out your yoga floor covering, tie up your running footwear or pump some iron-- whatever helps you and also feels good for your body!

3. Consume sufficient water

Stay clear of getting dehydrated, specifically when you consume alcohol a great deal of coffee in the office. Bring a big mug and load it at the water fountain, or bring a couple of large bottles of water with you to the office. Drink throughout the day, and you might observe you get fewer headaches!

4. Keep a journal

Gain from your experiences in life by examining them in a journal. Use your journal as a location where you can unload whatever is going on in your mind. As nobody reviews your journal, creating every little thing down can have the exact same result as pouring out your heart to a therapist. Get it out, and also you feel quickly better!

5. Consume vegetables and fruit

Vegetables and fruit are loaded with nutrients and vitamins, and will maintain your body healthy. Additionally, fruits are lights of power. Fried junk foods can make you feel sunken and also heavy right into the ground, whereas veggies and fruits make you really feel stimulated and can contribute to an excellent mood.

6. Love

Have you observed in how several ancient religious beliefs the god or siren of love was one of the major gamers, and also just how in one of today's major religious beliefs the divine being is typically seen as the lord of love? Infuse your actions with love, and also you will enhance your resonances and state of mind.

7. Be appreciative

This set ties back to keeping a diary. You can keep a gratefulness checklist in your journal, to make sure that you concentrate on the positive occasions in your life By highlighting the important things you feel happy for in your day-to-day life, you will certainly realize what you love about your life, have the ability to reinforce it, and maintain pumping up your state of mind.

8. Keep range in your life.

Absolutely nothing is as much of a drag to your mood as constantly following the exact same routine. Flavor things up a little bit. Try something new every weekend. See areas and areas in your city where you've never ever been previously. Cook up a meal you have never eaten, possibly from a nation you have actually never ever seen. The possibilities are endless, and they will all bring a smile to your face and improve your mood.

9. Use garments you like

Despite where you go, that you are going to see and also what you are going to do, outfit to look and be your finest self. Whenever you see on your own in the home window or mirror, you'll notice the effort you made in the morning, and you'll quickly lift your state of mind.

10. Usage crucial oils that you enjoy

Take a little bottle with a mix of your preferred essential oils liquified in some sweet almond oil and also demineralized water wherever you go, and spray this mixture on your wrists whenever you need a little pick-me-up. Make use of a burner in your house to diffuse an aroma you like, and also pump your mood.

11. Separate from the internet after a specific time during the night

It's so easy to get drawn right into the internet for hours on end-- even reducing into rest time-- however it can leave us drained and feeling worn out. You'll rest better, wake up feeling much better and raise your favorable state of mind overall.

12. Discover something brand-new every day

Just like your body requires wholesome food to be sustained, your mind requires continued challenges to go on evolving. To tickle your mind each day, see to it you learn something new daily. Beginning finding out a brand-new language, see inspiring TED talks, resolve a puzzle-- just see to it you utilize your brain every day. You'll feel fresh, you'll really feel that you are continuously expanding, and this will certainly raise your mood.

CONCLUSION

Some days staying favorable and upbeat can seem like an uphill battle. Maybe it was a stressful day at the workplace, a fight with a good friend, or perhaps simply an off day-- whatever it is, there are most definitely things you can do to improve your mood.

and it's no wonder tiffs can creep up on us so often. According to psycho therapist Guy Winch, writer of the book Emotional First Aid: Healing Rejection, Guilt, Failure, and Other Everyday Hurts, a bad mood can be triggered by anything from regret over failing to remember somebody's birthday celebration, to impressive jobs on our to do list, to not obtaining enough sort on a individual or essential Facebook share. Generally, humans are sensitive creatures, and it's not abnormal and even unusual for little things to get us in a funk.

While it's difficult to constantly maintain a favorable state of mind, it's worth keeping in mind which aspects can negatively impact your feelings and just how best to stay clear of those triggers. If you are really feeling down, think of something better and transportation on your own to a much better area, where you can get back to really feeling effective, perkier and also in control.

There's no factor a bad mood must wreck your day-- or even a section of your day. Oftentimes when we're down concerning something at the office or a small interpersonal problem, a quick boost is certainly within your understanding; you just require a conscious wish to really feel better and a desire to take a few conscious steps towards it.

And if you're finding that your reduced or poor moods are lasting longer than they should, or as if you can't appear to tremble them, never ever be afraid to reach out to an expert

DISCLAIMER

This book is not intended as a substitute for the medical advice of physicians. The reader should regularly consult a physician in matters relating to his/her health and particularly with respect to any symptoms that may require diagnosis or medical attention.

(Health, mood theraphy)

Do Not Go Yet; One Last Thing To Do

If you enjoyed this book or found it useful, I'd be very grateful if you'd post a short review on Amazon. Your support does make a difference, and I read all the reviews personally so I can get your feedback and make this book even better.

Thanks again for your support!

Printed in Great Britain
by Amazon